THIRD CHOICE

RICH, POOR OR HYPERCUBE

ERIC Y.F. LIM

PARTRIDGE

To order additional copies of this book, contact
Toll Free 800 101 2657 (Singapore)
Toll Free 1 800 81 7340 (Malaysia)
orders.singapore@partridgepublishing.com

www.partridgepublishing.com/singapore

"The ultimate goal of farming is not the growing of crops, but the cultivation of human beings."
Masanobu Fukuoka, Japanese Farm Philosopher

"The ultimate goal of shared property ownership is not rent-collecting / capital gain, but the cultivation of human beings in Sharing and Caring of the Commons."
Eric Y.F. Lim, Hypercube @ SOHOland

CONTENTS

Acknowledgements ix
Foreword xi

Chapter 1: Introduction 1
Chapter 2: The Great Good Place 7
Chapter 3: Live, Work, Travel, Learn, Play 11
Chapter 4: The Sharing Economy and the Commons 14
Chapter 5: Social Business / Social Enterprise 17
Chapter 6: Networked Community 19
Chapter 7: Owning a Social Franchise 22
Chapter 8: The Essence of a Local-Global-Cosmic
            Perspective 25
Chapter 9: Convergence of Crises 30
Chapter 10: A Lifestyle Alternative: From SOHO to
            ROLO 37
Chapter 11: Serving the Acronym Soup 40
Chapter 12: Live 43
Chapter 13: Work 45
Chapter 14: Travel 50
Chapter 15: Learn 53
Chapter 16: Play..55
Chapter 17: Experience & Transformation 58
Chapter 18: Life Transcendence and Life
            TranscenDANCE 59
Chapter 19: Hypercube as a Living Experiment for
            Systems Thinking...62

Chapter 20: Own It. Live It. Spread it..................................66

Chapter 21:The Third Choice: Rich, Poor or Hypercube......68

Chapter 22: Conclusion...70

Recent Blog Postings...71

Index...93

Appendix A..97

Appendix B..99

Appendix C..101

Appendix D..107

Appendix E..109

Appendix F...111

Appendix G.. 115

Appendix H.. 119

Appendix I...121

Appendix J...123

Appendix K..125

Appendix L..127

Endnotes.. 131

Bibliography...133

ACKNOWLEDGEMENTS

The author wishes to express his appreciations to various helps extended to this publishing effort, particularly the following individuals (in chronological sequence):

- *Amy Steele of San Diego, California, USA for editing the initial first draft.*
- *Kevin Weijers of Heemstede, Nederland for attempting simplification of the Hypercube concept.*
- *Angela Dietrich of London, U.K for reviewing the second draft.*
- *Dr. Al Wee, a fellow Malaysian, for frank discussion on the potential (and important caveats emphasized) of Blockchain Technology for tokenization of real property via ICO (Initial Coin Offering).*
- *Claudiane Reny of Montreal, Canada for third reading and finalizing the printer-ready version of this book.*

There were also many individuals who had knowingly or unknowingly contributed contents, ideas, photographs and videos mentioned in the book, resulting from the various activities carried out during the course of writing of this book.

Any mistakes /omissions yet to be rectified shall remain the sole responsibility of the author who also wishes to issue a Disclaimer that the Hypercube is still a working proto-type (but Open Source: copying is welcome and constitutes a most sincere form of compliment), and your participation and "pivoting and commoning" is most welcome, as we transition to the Sharing Economy / The Commons actively promoted in this book. However, any copying and duplicating / modifications of the proto-type, without our participation, is done at your own risks.

Foreword

Choices are often framed as bipolar: yes or no, black or white, rich or poor, thesis or anti-thesis. However, very often the best choice is a mixture of both or in-between. For instance, Synthesis comes from Thesis and Anti-thesis. Likewise, Po is in-between of Yes and No. Gray is derived from Black and White. Color Green comes from Yellow and Blue.

What is the in-between or Synthesis of Rich and Poor? It is the synthesis of Capitalism and Communism / Socialism. It is the Sharing Economy / The Commons / Communalism / Solidarity Economy or Collaborative Consumption and Peer-to-Peer Production.

It is the objective of this book to elaborate on this developing trend and to showcase a working prototype and business model... in the form of a "Hypercube" --- a multi-purpose "Shared" property or real estate that illustrates the Sharing Economy and Generative Ownership that is also a "Social Business"..... "Do Good. Make Money. Have Fun". As a starter, it is interesting and revealing to study the demographic profiles of the world.

Members of the Baby Boomer generation (born between 1946 to1964) enjoyed the benefits resulting from the economic development and growth after the Second World War. The socio-economic situations were relatively stable and conducive to growth and development and resulting prosperity. Being Middle Class / Rich / Super-rich became the aspiration (and hopefully the reality) for a substantial portion of the population. The resulting lifestyles and value systems have become the dominant and prevailing socio-economic model...

appropriately called Corporate Capitalism. This generation also saw the collapse of the other socio-economic systems called Communism / Socialism.

However, members of Generation-X (born between1965 to1984), Generation-Y (born between1985 to 2000 and also called Millennials) and even Generation-Z (born after 2000) come to face quite a different socio-economic environment. There are more uncertainties and instabilities, yet coupled with advances in information and communication technologies. Collectively, members of these new generations have the tendency to adopt a different lifestyle and values system. They prefer freedom, independence and mobility, and seeking a like-minded community, characterized by awareness of and concern with issues such as sustainability, personal development, business startup, disparity of wealth etc... appropriately called Community Capitalism which has the flavor of both Capitalism and Communalism / Socialism.

The other possible equivalent for Community Capitalism is Sharing Economy / Collaborative Consumption / Solidarity Economy. This is the Third Choice facing humanity in general and individuals in particular.

This book is a working exposition of the inner working of Sharing Economy / Collaborative Consumption / Solidarity Economy, particularly the following aspects: (1) The Great Socializer (curation of a community of autonomous and mobile people) (2) The Great Equalizer (overcoming the disparity in wealth and property ownership), in the form of hybrid space (known as Hypercube) for co-working and co-living, incorporating Live-Work-Travel-Learn-Play aspects of modern and holistic living.

Chapter 1: Introduction

Most of us would agree that one of the most valuable assets to every one of us is our personal space — a space where we feel free and alive, positive and meaningful. Personal space is usually viewed as psychological bubble surrounding us. It is actually much more than that. Our immediate physical and social environments constitute the bulk of the form and the content of our personal space.

This book expounds on the various ways and means to expand such physical and social environments, just as a Hypercube — a multi-dimensional and many-faceted cube — is an expanded version of the normal cube — a form with three dimensions only.

The Third Place

The third place has a special significance given by American urban sociologist Professor Ray Oldenburg, author of the influential book *The Great Good Place*. Oldenburg describes the third place, which he also calls "the great good place," as a social realm necessary to maintain a balanced life.[1] It's a space of social surrounding, separate from the two usual social environments of home — the first place — and the workplace — the second place.

A third place can be anything that serves the purpose of a social connection, a space with overlapping purposes and activities. In that sense, Facebook can be considered the largest third place in the world.

What is a "Hypercube"?

A hypercube is a 'third place' that has a physical structure and a virtual or social environment that serve the purpose of initiating and developing social connections, such as clubhouses (physical) or social clubs (non-physical). It can also function as a secondary residence with a business center. A hypercube is therefore a kind of "three-in-one" space.

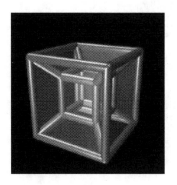

Yet it is a LEAN Property (Minimum acquisition cost but not low-cost, Maximum benefit or RICH functionally, socially, culturally and even spiritually). For the millennials or those who are nostalgic about their memorable days in school / college / varsity, a good way to visualize Hypercube / LEAN Property / Co-Living is to ask themselves the question "What is next after Student Accommodation?" The ideal answer could well be a Hypercube / LEAN Property / Co-Living space or similar.

What is next after Student Accommodation?

LEAN Property / Hypercube (Millennial Digital Nomads Hubs)

- *Meet Digital Nomads and enjoy FREE accommodations worldwide*
- *New Business Model (Sharing Economy): Co-working & Co-Living*
- *LEAN Property (co-owned Property Chain / Hypercubes)*
- *LEAN Startup business as Property Chain mini- tycoon*
- *Digital Nomad Lifestyle: Live-Work-Travel-Learn-Play*

While Facebook is a third place, it is not a hypercube since it lacks a physical structure or presence for living and working. Therefore a hypercube is a third place (and more), but not all third places can be a hypercube.

Live, Work, Travel, Learn, Play

Most of our daily lives revolve around living, working, traveling, learning and playing, referred to as "LWTLP." A Hypercube is designed to enhance the experience of personal space five-fold, by allowing its dwellers to explore each of these to the fullest. It's a residence, office, guesthouse, educational space, and a playground — all in one.

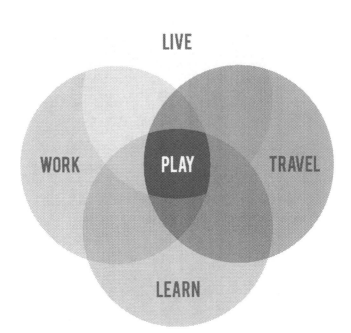

LIVE

WORK PLAY TRAVEL

LEARN

We are the incubator of such visualization, turning it into physical form in the shape of LEAN Property.

Incubator of LEAN Properties (精益房產)

- **LEAN PROPERTY:** *Minimum acquisition cost but not low-cost, maximum benefits (RICH Functionally, Socially, Culturally)*

- **LEAN COMMUNITY:** *Community of LEAN PROPERTIES and their owners and participants, including those who subscribe to the ideals of LEAN LOGIC (by Dr. David Fleming), The Sharing Economy / The Commons / Solidarity Economy etc.*

- **VILLAGE 3.0:** *We envisage places over-flowing with entrepreneurship, culture and innovation that also support holistic health, location independent livelihoods and the pursuit of lifelong learning. An ideal integration of Live-Work-Travel-Learn-Play eco-system*

The Triple Bottom Line

The concept of the Hypercube is social-environmental economics in real action. It complies fully with the triple-bottom-line (TBL) principle of profit, people and planet (3P), or economy, equity and environment (3E). The Hypercube initiative gives equal emphasis to 3P and 3E, with the former trending to people or community and the latter trending to equity or equality. Therefore, the brand of TBL we are talking about here is a blend of 3P and 3E.

The Hypercube is based on the sharing economy, otherwise known as the collaborative or solidarity economy. The space can be used to host anyone — tourists, couch-surfers, digital nomads, entrepreneurs or artists — and all join together to share in the LWTLP lifestyle, thus achieving the most efficient utilization of resources and spaces. The environmental impact of the Hypercube is minimal, since the formation, management and operation of the Hypercube is based on the sharing economy, with much less resource utilization and waste generation.

Simultaneously, this type of third space is a business. It can be an opportunity to practice lean startup — using low costs and minimal staff to launch any business idea — in your very own space with a team of collaborators. It's a social enterprise addressing a specific social problem: house ownership among a disadvantaged segment of the population who face the mounting pressure of inflation.

Whether you're driven by exploring a new business venture (profit/economy), participating in a collaborative social space (people/equity), or positively impacting the earth (planet/environment), the Hypercube @ SOHOland covers all three — and so much more.

The SOHO Concept

Tom Atlee articulates the idea behind the Hypercube in a comment posted to his blog, <u>Random Communications from an Evolutionary Edge</u>, on July 28, 2009:

Conceptually, SOHO is an interesting concept within which to pull together many transformational approaches — including permaculture and other green/sustainability perspectives, triple bottom line (and corporate social responsibility), generational shifts, "glocalization," the Web, holistic philosophy, and personal well-being and development — all in an entrepreneurial context. My parallel effort to pull such things together under the concept of "co-intelligence" has had a process/democracy center of gravity (rather than a business one).

Chapter 2: The Great Good Place

On first sight, the term "third place" sounds belittling ("not even in second place?"). On the contrary, actually third places are the great good places. Third places are "social condensers."

A social condenser, according to Dom Nozzi, is "the place where citizens of a community or neighbourhood meet to develop friendships, discuss issues, and interact with others." They're important in the way a community develops a sense of identity and maintains cohesion.[2]

In *The Great Good Place*, Ray Oldenburg calls these locations third places — the first being the home and the second being the workplace. These third places are crucial for a number of reasons, according to Oldenburg.[3] They provide a sense of community, they encourage a nurturing of social relationships, and they're spaces where people can relax and unwind in an informal way.

Power of Ten

A good source to obtain information, advice and guidance on placemaking is Project for Public Spaces (PPS), a nonprofit dedicated to helping people create and sustain public spaces that build up communities.

PPS created a concept, called the Power of 10+, that tells us that a space succeeds if people have 10 or more reasons to be there. Cities need 10+ destinations, destinations need 10+ places, and places need 10+ activities. Successful owners, managers and operators of third places follow this rule of the Power of 10+.[4]

Co-working facilities are considered third places *and* public places, just like many other commercial enterprises established for these purposes. An effective co-working space can also follow the Power of 10+ concept by incorporating live, work, travel, learn, and play values.

The SOHO Paradigm

A small office/home office (SOHO) offers the convenience of an office in every home, either for a business startup (part-time or full-time) or management of personal and family matters in a business-like manner.

The following three objectives are key to the small office/home office (SOHO) paradigm:

- business/enterprise development
- personal/family development
- social and ecosystem development

The three main objectives can be found across all variations of the SOHO paradigm, including the following:

- mobile office/home office (MOHO): another version of SOHO, except mobility is given a more important role, such as greater use of smart-phones, etc.
- co-working facilities and services (COWO): the sharing of office facilities and services to minimize cost outlays
- intentional community and co-housing (COHO): the sharing of living spaces or house-sharing
- cooperation commons (COCO): another way to share working or housing facilities via a cooperative setup

run in accordance with cooperative laws or based on the practice of the commons (please see below).

Although the above are not necessarily linear and sequential, the listed order could be convenient and useful for discussion purposes, particularly if we are to view them in the context of business development, personal development, and social and ecosystem development according to the triple-bottom-line principle of profit, people and planet, or economy, equity and environment.

In fact, an innovative and fully functional business model incorporating the three objectives and five variations listed above would be the ultimate perspective and goal of the SOHO paradigm.

The Art and Science of Placemaking

SOHO can also mean "sociable home," and it extends the concept of the third place even further to incorporate "the commons."

The commons is a space plus "a resource *plus* a defined community *and* the protocols, values and norms devised by the community to manage its resources," according to David Bollier.[5] The concept of the commons is also extensively utilized by having a subscription-, membership- or shareholder-based community.

Placemaking, the practice of creating or making places, is an art and science used when designing a home or work space. The formation and operation of a sociable home — such as the Hypercube — naturally involves placemaking. The Hypercube incorporates the concept of a first place, a home-share or co-housing; a second space, a co-working business center; and a third space, a social condenser or the commons.

In short, the practice of placemaking, with a high value placed on the commons, is fully incorporated in the concept of the sociable home, aka the Hypercube.

Chapter 3: Live, Work, Travel, Learn, Play

The 21st century is witnessing the emergence of the new normal: the sharing economy, collaborative consumption, and the solidarity economy. This is impacting companies and their employees, particularly in terms of the advocacy for the triple-bottom-line (TBL) principle of profit, people and planet, or economy, equity and environment. Companies, employees and people in general are starting to focus not only on money but also on adopting sustainable and healthier lifestyles which should have the elements of Live, Work, Travel, Learn, Play or (LWTLP) as a holistic ecosystem.

The Hypercube is conceived for the LWTLP lifestyle, and its ecosystem is designed as a social business to promote the sharing economy. A co-working and co-housing or co-living space normally develops a social commons based on shared equity, environmental conservation, and open cooperativism.

The LWTLP lifestyle, as it is reflected in the Hypercube, can be summarized as follows:

- Live: The Hypercube is a third place that can also function as a primary residence or second home or home-stay for travelers or digital nomads
- Work: People can use the Hypercube for telework, as a business incubator and as an accelerator to grow a business.
- Travel: The space can be used to host visitors for a holiday swap.

- Learn: Since people with a variety of backgrounds use the Hypercube, it has potential for skills exchanges and workshops.
- Play: It can be a space for recreation, relaxation and meaningful and transcendental moments with different people.

A transition to the sharing economy is done through space sharing, tool sharing and skill-sharing etc. A collaborative second home — with its LWTLP components — is designed to reflect this emerging global trend. The principle behind it is based on collaborative consumption, a practical way of sharing resources for both consumption and production.

By owning and/or sharing a collaborative second home, you may be able to adopt a new and healthier lifestyle in accordance with the TBL, which will bring benefits not only for yourself but also for those around you.

A collaborative second home uses innovative ideas about spaces, combined with professional management and democratic control. The Hypercube expands on this, creating specialized and dedicated areas for entertainment, learning, socializing and working. It truly integrates the LWTLP concept in one location — creating an integral or holistic lifestyle.

The Hypercube enhances both the capital and rental values of the property, as it acts as a valuable extension to its residents' homes and improves the quality of life of the occupants in many ways.

Using collaborative consumption, the Hypercube allows for a culture of sharing, openness, and sustainability. By becoming part of a collaborative second home, you will own an economic engine that also takes care of its people and the planet. This is full compliance of the various principles highlighted in LEAN

Logic (by Dr. David Fleming), briefly summarized below (thus qualifying Hypercube as "LEAN Property"):

- Act on smallest scale possible with the maximum participation and benefit
- Small is beautiful / Sustainability / Resilience
- Small-scale community is our default pattern for resilience / survival
- Not "de-growth" but "de-intensification"
- Closed and circular system
- Vision of Civility for a world in trouble
- Viable social and economic blueprint in the Nature context
- Joyful Play
- Play is one of the core themes

Chapter 4: The Sharing Economy and the Commons

The commons, according to Wikipedia, is the "cultural, intellectual and natural resources accessible to members of society without any individual having exclusive ownership. Such resources are in common beneficial use by a group, which may be two people or the entire population of the world."[6] This definition, however, doesn't deal with "managed common" (with the "private ownership" component and associated management) and "unmanaged common, (without any "private ownership" and hence not "managed" at all"). The managed commons, manifested through the sharing economy, is crucial for the success of the Hypercube. This is also the Third Choice.

The Hypercube is based on the idea of "commoning," which is derived from "the commons" and means sharing resources in a fashion that allows all of society to have an equal part and say in the usage of these resources.

It's the act of "people self-organizing to co-produce and co-govern resources that they recognize as important for their livelihood and well-being," according to Commons Rising, a group dedicated to connecting people with the commons.[7] These resources can be physical or knowledge-based. A common is formed by a resource and the act of commoning, which defines our relationship with the resource. Projects such as Couchsurfing, Uber, hackerspaces, P2P, Airbnb and other forms of co-working, office, ride or farmland sharing are all examples of commoning.

David Bollier, in his blog post "The Commons, Short and Sweet," writes: "The commons is a social system for the long-term stewardship of resources that preserves shared values and community identity." He describes it as follows:

The commons is a self-organized system by which communities manage resources (both depletable and and replenishable) with minimal or no reliance on the Market or State. [The commons is] the wealth that we inherit or create together and must pass on, undiminished or enhanced, to our children. Our collective wealth includes the gifts of nature, civic infrastructure, cultural works and traditions, and knowledge. [It's] a sector of the economy (and life!) that generates value in ways that are often taken for granted — and often jeopardized by the Market-State.

There is no master inventory of commons because a commons arises whenever a given community decides it wishes to manage a resource in a collective manner, with special regard for equitable access, use and sustainability.

The commons is not a resource. It is a resource *plus* a defined community *and* the protocols, values and norms devised by the community to manage its resources. Many resources urgently need to be managed as commons, such as the atmosphere, oceans, genetic knowledge and biodiversity.

There is no commons without commoning — the social practices and norms for managing a resource for collective benefit. Forms of commoning naturally vary from one commons to another because humanity itself is so varied. And so there is no "standard template" for commons; merely "fractal affinities" or shared patterns and principles among commons. The commons must be understood, then, as a verb as much as a noun. A commons must be animated by bottom-up participation, personal responsibility, transparency and self-policing accountability[8].

This is the ideal behind the establishment and operation of the Hypercube project initiative.

Chapter 5: Social Business / Social Enterprise

Non-profit organizations deal with social issues rather than commercial or business issues. Since they're social entities, not commercial entities, they usually depend on the generosity of the public or private sectors for funding and growth. Their mode of operation is, therefore, not self-sustainable.

However, there is now a trend for such organizations to become self-sustainable through adopting a business-like approach while still serving its social function or mission. Such modified or new entities are collectively known as social businesses, placing great emphasis on the triple bottom line (TBL) of profit, people and planet, or economy, equity, and environment.

Social businesses will evolve into social enterprises when they go even beyond TBL and have a longer term perspective with more emphasis on developmental outcomes or impacts than mere growth in economic outputs.

The Hypercube functions as a social business to promote the sharing economy via co-working and co-housing. As a business, it promotes the live, work, travel, learn, play lifestyle to develop a social commons.

To ensure project sustainability and continual participation, the objective is to achieve the social experience of "Do good. Make money. Have fun." The Hypercube strives to overcome, both locally and globally, the following social and economic problems currently faced by people around the globe:

- inability to own a primary home
- declining job market
- wealth inequality or distribution, particularly in the property market

By providing a mechanism for co-housing (a shared home) on a shared ownership basis, the threshold for property investment is lowered substantially. Shared ownership allows most people to join the game, rather than being excluded from participation. Co-housing is a solution for those suffering from the consequence of high inflation in property prices, which are forever rising faster than wages.

Furthermore, the co-working arrangement (a shared office) can encourage and support entrepreneurship or lean business startups among job-seekers, providing an alternative route to a declining job market. Ideally, people should be independent rather than merely depending on conventional employment for income.

Most importantly, the redistribution of income and wealth brought about by such a mechanism would remove or eliminate disparity in society, achieving social equity and solidarity via collaborative consumption within the sharing economy.

The Hypercube is an example of open cooperativism, entrepreneurship and the commons, thus bringing about needed social changes, particularly in housing and home ownership. It was conceived as a working prototype of the sharing economy — promoting a sense of solidarity and fraternity in the property sector — to achieve the triple bottom line.

Chapter 6: Networked Community

With costs spiraling, it's been hard for young people to buy houses. Compounding the situation is the uncertain economic environment that makes well-paid jobs hard to come by. Even business startups are risky propositions in case of a lack of social networks and an alienating lifestyle.

The following are the root causes for these socio-economic problems:

- inflation working against average salary-workers
- escalating costs of residential properties
- startup costs for a new business
- lack of relevant knowledge and guidance
- the middle-income trap
- logistical difficulties with a business startup
- lack of opportunity to form social groups/living an alienating lifestyle
- lack of a holistic lifestyle

The solution to these socio-economic problems lies in a totally different approach to work: a networked community based on the sharing economy.

The Hypercube is a viable alternative to traditional views of earning a living. It promotes early house ownership and comes with a business proposal that could be operated on a part-time basis, with the prospect of turning into something really big, yet socially and environmentally compatible.

The Hypercube gives you a home, a business and a network.

Jessica Reeder, in her article "Hacking Home: Coliving Reinvents the Commune for a Networked Age," expands further on co-living: "The underlying concept of co-living will be nothing new to anyone who has roommates … [It's] a new type of cohabitation" that balances work and life. "Here, 'home' is reinvented with a new purpose. It's a community, an ethos, a series of opportunities for collaboration." Co-living, she writes, infuses "the blurring boundaries of work and leisure with new opportunities for inspiration, learning and social innovation."

Co-working — joining individual professionals in one common workspace — influences co-living. "With no boss, no distractions and a building full of inspiring peers, synergy is the quick result of this separate-yet-together environment," she writes.

Taking that a step further, a co-living home creates even stronger connections. Like-minded people share a common lifestyle and vision of the world. "Co-living spaces develop unique cultures based on the location and people chosen, their mission statement, and house activities," Reeder writes. "The underlying culture gives birth to serendipitous connections between residents who share similar values and passions." It is an example of networked individualism, and "inspired entrepreneurism is a central tenet."

"Contemporary co-living builds on communal living practices, embracing a networked tech, business and science-fueled culture built upon innovation and realizing a better world through collaborative design," she writes. It's "entrepreneurialism with a conscience."

Co-living isn't exclusive, but its results are magical. "It connects people in a multitude of ways, building trust and creating infinite opportunities for collaboration," she writes.

Imagine the ultimate: an international co-living network. "Imagine having a home wherever you go, well-appointed and populated by people you truly enjoy. Imagine landing in a new city and having an extensive professional network already in place," she writes.

"Much of this is related to the 21st-century vision of sharing, which allows for a high level of individualism and experimentation," Reeder says. "The co-living movement seeks out exceptional people, asking them not to give themselves up to a single cause, but to support each other's exceptionality. This may be the key to a new definition of 'home,' one which provides comfort and friends along with inspiration and innovation."[9]

The Hypercube is all about living within a functional sharing economy — co-working, co-living and sharing an inspiring life with others.

Chapter 7: Owning a Social Franchise

The Hypercube business model is designed for organic growth in a collaborative manner. It's a social business. It's your opportunity to practice lean startups in your very own incubator with a team of collaborators. Participation in the Hypercube project is to join a community of like-minded people who are looking for a new way to live, work, travel, learn and play.

The "3+1 Plan"

Initially, a participant will jointly own (with two other investors) a single Hypercube in a chosen location. This will be the participant's base station. The participant will then duplicate a new Hypercube by getting three new participants to jointly own it. The process may be duplicated many times to form a Hypercube cluster. This is the "3+1 Plan." The numbers represent three original first-tier investors plus the first Hypercube.

The 3+1 Plan is the essence of the social franchise that will expand the Hypercube concept, locally, regionally and globally. It is the mechanism which will drive the co-housing and co-living movement.

Easy and early house ownership via the Hypercube beats an inflationary and uncertain socio-economic environment, while building up a franchise in property investment with a community. This is the sharing economy at its best.

Here's how it works:

1. You enter into a lease-purchase option on a property of your choice.
2. You convert the lease into a purchase at your convenience.
3. You choose a business startup (or use the social franchise built into the Hypercube cluster concept).
4. You become a full member of the Co-living Co-working Community (CCC).
5. You duplicate the process and form more CCCs of your own (the "3+1 Plan").
6. You finally own a chain of properties and a thriving social business.

The essence of the Hypercube social franchise offers a home, business and network of like-minded people participating in the sharing economy.

Yet another channel to expand the Hypercube initiative is to work with property developers. The Hypercube could be widely incorporated into existing or future condominium projects or housing estates. Joint ventures with, or sponsorship by, property developers or other stakeholders would create a win-win situation.

Target Audiences:
Serving the Millennials & the
Third Agers (Retirees)

Millenial Generation

- Overcoming the new "Homelessness" via sharing
- Transiting from Traditional Education to Experiential Education (LWTLP)
- Transiting from Employment to Entrepreneurship
- Digital Nomas (Freedom & Mobility) Via Blockchains (like Bitcoin and Bitcars)

The 3rd Ager Generation

- New lifestyle: Third Age & Second Life
- Overcoming retirement blues
- Health / Wealth / Happiness
- Self-Actualization & Maturity
- Developping Passion and Compassion
- Creating legacy: Social Entrepreneur

Chapter 8: The Essence of a Local-Global-Cosmic Perspective

The global crises happening now worldwide are closely related to the issue of sustainability. Sustainability in itself cannot be properly addressed without taking a simultaneously global and local view. This involves our personal work-life balance in the context of social and ecological concerns and responsibilities. We need a framework to put all these issues in a coherent manner. This is done through the introduction of the SOHO taxonomy:

- local: small office/home office (SOHO-1)
- global: Solar Heliospheric Observatory (SOHO-2)
- cosmic: self-organizing holarchical open system (SOHO-3)
- commons: sociable home (SOHO-4)

SOHO-1 deals with earning a living and achieving higher productivity through working at home or in the office, especially in small office home office. This is very much "local" stuff. The Plan-Do-Check-Act (PDCA) Cycle, which was made popular by Dr. W. Edwards Deming, is used in SOHO-1 to bring about optimal productivity, innovation and creativity. The PDCA Cycle determines how effectively and efficiently we earn our living. The promotion of entrepreneurship in the form of SOHO-1 is also very much encouraged.

This is the *economy*, or the *profit*, part of the triple bottom line (TBL) principle. It is essentially acting locally. This will improve our quality of working.

SOHO-2 concerns the tracking of the solar activities that have direct effects on the atmospheric conditions of Earth, thus affecting the climate world-wide. This is very much "global" stuff. The permaculture cycle advocates the global approach in solving local problems (the so-called re-localization movement), while emphasizing diversity, resilience and harmony. The complexity of the environment is well-respected and the conservation of energy practiced. The role of the sun, and the associated Solar Heliospheric Observatory (SOHO-2) spacecraft, is well acknowledged, confirming the need for worldwide re-solarization efforts — such as installing solar panels and planting trees.

This is the *environmental*, or the *planetary*, part of the TBL principle. It is essentially thinking globally. This will improve our quality of living.

SOHO-3 seems to be the universal organizing principle of the universe, giving rise to life and intelligence in our universe, seemingly against the "entropy" effect. This is very much "cosmic" stuff. The holon cycle, a reference to the self-organizing holarchical open (SOHO-3) system, emphasizes the interconnectedness and interdependence of things and beings in the cosmos, via the holarchy structure rather than hierarchy structure. Everything is "always partial, already whole" or a "box-in-a-box-in-a-box." We are all interconnected and interdependent.

This is the *equity*, or the *people*, part of the TBL principle. It is essentially connecting cosmically. This will improve our quality of life.

SOHO-4 represents a framework for the evolution of thinking about the various socio-economic, environmental and political trends in the world. The commons are likely to be the most favored solution to many problems facing mankind.

Sociable Homes (SOHO-4) are commons prototypes and serve as a transition to the new paradigm.

The Hypercube is, therefore, an attempt to realize such commons, locally, globally and spiritually.

GRP Meets GBP

The Hypercube is comprised of a grass-roots philosophy (GRP) — essentially made up of economically disadvantaged local individuals — and the global business plan (GBP) — intended to expand locally, regionally and globally through the built-in "social franchise" (see details in **Chapter 7: Owning a Social Franchise**). These give prominence to soil, sun and soul, which lead to health, wealth and happiness, via social and environmental entrepreneurship based on the TBL principle.

The GRP is a grass-roots approach commencing with a business start-up from a small office/home office (SOHO-1). The approach creates spare time to engage in astronomy, studying the Solar Heliospheric Observatory (SOHO-2), which may further extend our investigation into the self-organizing holarchical open (SOHO-3) system. Eventually, this helps us answer life's big questions such as "Why there is life?" and "What is the purpose of life?"

The GBP, on the other hand, involves having an office in every home for each and every one of us, as a launch-pad for a business venture. The goal is to be a fully-fledged social and environmental entrepreneur, someone who can transition to localization (or re-localization) as an alternative to conventional capitalism. Hopefully this will lead many of us to financial independence, as free agents of Generation-E — a generation that values environment, energy, equity, enterprise, emotion and e-commerce.

The word "global" has two connotations: (1) taking all stakeholders into consideration and integrating LWTLP and (2) being applicable and extendible to all countries and nations, useable by everyone wishing to become part of Generation-E.

Personal and Business Enlightenment

The path to personal and business enlightenment, which consists in many small steps, could be broadly described as three steep flights of stairs:

1. survival: manageability of prevailing situations (or profit/economy for business under the triple-bottom-line [TBL] principle)
2. understanding: comprehensibility of the phenomena (or planet/environment for business under the TBL)
3. wisdom and love: meaningfulness of various encounters (or people/equity for business under the TBL)

Manageability, comprehensibility and meaningfulness will give us a sense of coherence, which is a source of our health and wellbeing. This is the essence of the thesis of Salutogenesis, the term first used and promulgated by Aaron Antonovsky in 1979, in the context of alternative medicine. Antonovsky essentially posits that quality of life (more than just quality of living) is dependent on understanding and experiencing this very sense of integration and coherence. Any holistic solution includes a local, global and cosmic aspect — to "think globally, act locally, connect cosmically."

Individual Responsibility

Individually, we might have to earn our keep by making better and more efficient use of a SOHO-1. We might have to produce a portion of our food by having a better understanding of permaculture in particular, and of ecology, in general. We should better recognize the importance of the sun, partly through the SOHO-2.

Corporate Responsibility

Corporation-wise, managers might have to get a quick grasp of the differences among hierarchy, holarchy and panarchy, the essence of which is better understood by studying the behavior of holons (SOHO-3).

Armed and equipped with these four types of SOHO, we would then have the physical, scientific and philosophical / spiritual basis to strengthen our faith in the Hypercube initiative in face of the challenging times ahead.

We need a vehicle to demonstrate the essence and the operation of these ingredients together, which can be local-global-cosmic or body-mind-spirit systems thinking (see Chapter 20: Own It. Live It. Spread it.). This vehicle is the envisaged Hypercube in the form of a sociable home (SOHO-4). It's meant to establish a community of like-minded people dedicated to this ideal, leading to the formation of the commons.

Chapter 9: Convergence of Crises

There is a clear indication of a forthcoming convergence of global crises or the 8F Crises: fuel, food, finance, family, faith, fertility (soil and population), fluidity and fellowship.

- Fuel: Energy derived from various forms of fuel is the driving force of the modern economy and civilization. Depletion of petroleum resources calls for drastic actions from all sectors. Alternative forms of the energy supply must be urgently sourced and efficiently used.
- Food: Security of food supply covers the sufficiency (quantity), sustainability (long-term) and safety (health) aspects. There are no countries in the world having a viable long-term solution for this problem yet.
- Finance: Financial and monetary issues are constantly causing disruptions and upheavals throughout the world, resulting in great disparity and inequality.
- Family: The connection to one's family is diminishing in many parts of the world.
- Faith: The role of spirituality is under threat as more and more people lack a cosmic or transcendent perspective.
- Fertility: The depletion of soil fertility threatens the survival of humanity, compounded by a drop in fertility rates in many developed countries and increasing rates in developing countries, causing grave concern in long-term demographic profiles.
- Fluidity: Air and water pollution problems, the changing oceanic tidal waves, flooding and huge climatic turbulence are due to global warming.

- Fellowship: No man is an island. Yet the world is lacking this very sense of camaraderie, which can only be realized through genuine networked communities.

Very often we look for solutions to these 8F crises by employing just external considerations, as if the solution lies outside of us. Actually, the real solution lies within each and every one of us in the way we live, work, travel, learn and play, starting with our small office home office.

What Is the Future of Work?

Think about how the future economy will really function, with the coming of the end of cheap oil, global environmental pollution, climate change, and soil fertility loss. How will these crises impact people's lives and what are some possible changes to our lifestyle and values systems?

We are all looking for a fine balance of home, work and life, especially in face of the coming convergence of fuel, food and finance crises. We all need to consider a plan B — and sooner than we think.

Quality of Life

The determination of the quality of life in cities can only be measured by considering comprehensively where and how we live, work and earn a living, and relating this to life in its totality. This fine balance of home, work and life is the essence of quality of life and is a highly individual matter that keeps changing throughout our respective tenures on Earth as we pass through different phases of our lives.

However, there are certain common factors that we all look for such as safety and security, sustainability and resilience, health and happiness, and value of time and nature. This leads us to the practice of a lifestyle of health and sustainability (LOHAS) and its merger with the slow movement, forming what can be called the slow lifestyle of happiness and sustainability (SLOHAS).

The 21st century will witness the global-scale transformation of towns and cities toward SLOHAS as citizens worldwide try to seek a fine balance in the home-work-life matrix in their attempts to get a better quality of life.

The Hypercube is an incubator for such transition to SLOHAS through its opportunities for social-environmental entrepreneurship development. The Hypercuber bridges the digital divide and encourages energy efficiency due to its extensive promotion of information and communications technology (ICT) skills and social networking.

City-dwellers and the Co-working Space

Co-working facilities and services — a shared office space, WiFi access and meeting and conference rooms, for example — are targeted primarily to improve the socio-economic status of certain city-dweller groups in a sustainable manner. The following groups seek opportunities for collaboration, synergy and solidarity and could benefit from participating in the Hypercube.

Beneficiaries	Descriptions
Stay-at-home parents	These are parents looking for work-from-home business opportunities, while looking after children and family. Skills acquisition is also an important consideration for this demographic.
Recent Graduates	This demographic is typically younger... those seeking self-employment, guidance and mentorship, networking and collaboration.
Retrenched Workers	Retrenched workers are those starting a second career via green business opportunities (such as any chemical-free or organic venture or green way of living), with minimum capital, while leading a new LOHAS lifestyle.
Retirees	Third-agers looking for a second career (voluntary or otherwise) that will turn their past experience and connections into unique advantages, such as consulting, book authorship etc.
Down-Shifters	Persons who are powering down to a SLOHAS pace in their career path.

The Hypercube will result not only in a better city, but also in a better life for these groups, in the form of vibrant LOHAS and SLOHAS sectors.

Solutions to the 8F Crises

What is the next convergence of crisis and what more could be done? There are many possible solutions to be incorporated, which will be highlighted as a soup of acronyms and abbreviations somewhat linked to — and taking advantage of — the tremendous recall value of the well-known giants in the digital world: IBM, ICT and Apple. These abbreviations emphasize the important role of digital tools and social media in social-environmental enterprises, as well as the importance of biotechnology and carbon in the overall scheme of things.

Operationally, the proposed project would strive for a combination of ICT and an environmental approach, giving prominence to new hybrids distinct from the original version or entities: IBM 2.0, ICT 2.0 and APPLE 2.0.

IBM 2.0 (representing Incubator + Biotech + Media, what the emerging new world really needs):

- incubators/accelerators for lean business startups that encourage the development of entrepreneurship in the developed and developing countries
- biotechnology that will address the various issues connected with food safety and security, medical sciences, etc.
- media literacy and the proper utilization of the Internet for propagation / dissemination of information and knowledge, etc.

ICT 2.0 (representing Internet + Carbon + Transition):
- Internet (and possibly a more advanced version in the future) as the core of the new carbon and the emission of CO2, which remains the central issue confronting mankind, the economy and the new world
- the role of biochar (biological charcoal) as the possible savior of humanity
- transition and the transition town movement — communities built around sustainable living — as a dominant theme for the forth-coming new world

APPLE 2.0 (representing Alliance for Post Petroleum Local Economy):

- The Alliance for Post Petroleum Local Economy is a grass-roots citizens' forum that works to become more sustainable and localized. Similar grass-roots organizations are P2P Foundation (www.p2pfoundation.net), Enspiral (www.enspiral.com), Las Indias (english.lasindias.com), Sensorica (www.sensorica.co) and Ethos (www.ethosvo.org).

- local economy, re-localization, and re-solarization (solar energy and reforestation) as important topics in a post-petroleum economy, local economy and P2P movement.

We need a new approach to mitigate the effects of the 8F Crises. We need a systems thinking approach, as illustrated by the permaculture methodology (and other systemic methods to be discussed in Chapter 19). It should be fully compatible with, or even exceeding, the expectations of the much publicized Green New Deal (under President Barack Obama) and the New Deal (under President Franklin Roosevelt).

People can work together to create their own solutions to the 8F crises as well by doing the following:

- Applying corporate social responsibility by using the triple bottom line to advocate for profit, people and planet, and economy, equity and environment.
- Introducing permaculture. Permanent agriculture, or sustainable agriculture, meets permanent culture, or a sustainable design or lifestyle, in this buzz word for a comprehensive design science. It mimics the workings of nature and promotes a sustainable future to counter

the devastating effects of the inevitable arrival of Peak Oil, when petroleum supplies run out.

- Promoting permaculture as an all-inclusive approach. Permaculture as a design science and a lifestyle or values system places particular emphasis on diversity and unity. In fact, it is an all-inclusive approach based on the workings of nature that will help overcome the adverse effects of the convergence of crisis.

There is even a tendency to use the noun "permaculture" as a verb to indicate its holistic approach, as exemplified in phrases like "permaculture everything" and "permablitz everyone," meaning to permaculturize everything and preach permaculture to everyone. It's similar to how "tweet" has become a new verb through Twitter.

The Hypercube project initiative is such an experiment for systems thinking, systems being, and systems living, very much like the Permaculture approach cited above (see Chapter 19).

Chapter 10: A Lifestyle Alternative: From SOHO to ROLO

The evolution of the Hypercube is designed around the various stages of life of a typical person living anywhere in the world: the lifecycle of schooling and learning, working, traveling, experiencing, retiring and mentoring.

The Hypercube provides the most valuable personal space for life-long engagement in the form of small office/home office or sociable home, both referred to as SOHO. It enables the pursuit of lean business startups and collaboration with various parties to form networks.

It can also serve as a retirement office/life office (ROLO) for those planning retirement and commencing an encore career. A ROLO be further treated as constituting two broad approaches:

- retirement office: planning for retirement and beginning a second career
- life office: mentoring young adults in personal development and career paths, for a complete realization of body, mind and spirit

Both kinds of SOHO and ROLO, as offered by the Hypercube, lead to a free, active and meaningful life. The Hypercube is, therefore, an evolutionary path towards the fulfilment of the following aims:

1. small office/home office
2. sociable home
3. retirement office/life office

It begins with the shared-ownership of a second or secondary home and continue through life to a meaningful and active retirement, all the while incorporating LWTLP values. The Hypercube can be your most valuable personal space, whatever your current life stage. It is designed to evolve from SOHO to ROLO, covering the complete life spectrum, in a fun, free and fulfilling way.

Most Powerful Personal Space

Hypercube will turn out to be (already endorsed by hundreds of references) your Most Powerful Personal Space:

(1) LEAN Property (co-owned property chain: incomes & capital gains)

(2) Live-Work-Travel-Learn-Play ecosystem (holistic lifestyle)

(3) LEAN Startup (your own ready-made social business)

Encore Careers

The ROLO aspects are very much less emphasized due to the non-glamorous nature of the issues involved. This really should not be the case. In fact, there are numerous issues connected with retirement and life planning that should be highlighted in order to tap the tremendous skills, knowledge, experience and wisdom that only this age group could provide.

In this regard, it may be very relevant to look closely at non-profit organizations such as encore.org, which, according to its website, "advances the idea of leveraging the skills and talents of experienced adults to improve communities and the world." The organization notes that an "encore" or "encore career" is "continued work in the second half of life that combines social impact, purpose, and often, continued income."

Life Planning

Life office or life planning, on the other hand, places emphasis on the various issues connected with the whole spectrum of the cycle of life: family planning, bringing up children, education choices, career development and self-actualization, savings and investments, life insurance, tax avoidance, retirement, travel, health maintenance, estate planning, gifts and charities, legacies, etc.

Even the issues concerning the purpose and meaning of life, wellbeing and happiness would crop up for consideration and deliberation. These could be spiritual and philosophical, but they're necessary in our pursuit of the pot of gold at the end of the rainbow.

Chapter 11: Serving the Acronym Soup

SoLoMo: Social, Local and Mobile

The terms social, local and mobile are widely used in information and communications technology, or ICT, particularly with the prevalence of mobile smart phones. However, the SoLoMo Manifesto, as applied in the design of the Hypercube, is a totally new version. It is a mixture of ingredients that yield the following:

- a social enterprise that takes into consideration the triple-bottom-line (TBL) principle of profit, people and planet, or economy, equity and environment
- local property in the form of a single apartment/condo-share/home-away-from-home that any person can OWN and LIVE in collaboratively
- a mobile lifestyle that provides escape from the dreaded 9-5 routine, achievable through lean business start-ups for fun, freedom, and fulfillment
- sustainable integration of the LWTLP lifestyle
- facilities that provide the means, tools and network required to attain the perfect state, in an ecologically friendly, socially equitable and financially sustainable way

SOMO: Social Property and Mobile Lifestyle

The objective of the SOMO Initiative, based on the principle of the sharing economy, is two-fold:

(1) Promotion of shared ownership of property as a great equalizer: The social objective is to enable the disadvantaged to own property collaboratively, thus overcoming disparities of wealth.

(2) Promotion of a mobile lifestyle in the holistic format of LWTLP: The mobile lifestyle objective (not just 9-5 jobs) improves economic well-being and is a great socializer with a community of like-minded people, i.e., own it and live it for fun, freedom and fulfillment.

SOHO1: Small Office/Home Office

Using the usual toolkit of productivity, innovations and creativity (such as the PDCA Cycle), the promotion of entrepreneurship in the form of SOHO1 is very much encouraged.

This is the *economy*, or the *profit*, part of the TBL principle. It is essentially acting locally. This will improve our quality of working.

SOHO2: Solar Heliospheric Observatory

The permaculture cycle advocates for the global approach in solving local problems (the so-called re-localization movement), while emphasizing diversity, resilience and harmony. The complexity of the environment is well-respected and the conservation of energy practiced. The role of the sun, and the associated Solar Heliospheric Observatory (SOHO2) spacecraft, is well acknowledged, confirming the need for worldwide re-solarization efforts — such as installing solar panels and planting trees. This is the *environment*, or the *planet*, part of the TBL principle. It is essentially thinking globally and will improve our quality of living.

SOHO3: Self-Organizing Holarchical Open System

The holon cycle, a reference to the self-organizing holarchical open (SOHO3) system emphasizes the interconnectedness and interdependence of things and beings in the cosmos via the holarchy structure rather than hierarchy structure. Everything is "always partial, already whole" or a "box-in-a-box-in-a-box." We are interconnected and interdependent.

This is the *equity*, or the *people*, part of the TBL principle. It is essentially connecting cosmically and will improve our quality of life.

SOHO1 deals with earning a living through working. This is very much "local" stuff. SOHO2 concerns the tracking of solar activities, which have a direct effect on the atmospheric conditions of Mother Earth, thus affecting the climatic conditions worldwide. This is very much "global" stuff. SOHO3 seems to be the organizing principle of the universe, giving rise to life and intelligence. This is very much "cosmic" stuff.

SOHO4: Sociable Home

SOHO4 is the evolution of thinking about the various socio-economic, environmental and political trends in the world. The "commons" are likely to be the most favored solution to many of the problems facing mankind. Sociable homes are "commons" prototypes and serve as a transition to the new paradigm.

Chapter 12: Live

Conventional thinking is thus: when you buy a house to live in, it is regarded as consumption; when you buy a house to rent out, it is regarded as investment; when you buy two houses or more, it is regarded as anti-social hoarding or speculation.

However, there is a socially and politically correct way to own a series of houses that is also environmentally and financially sound and smart. It's the sharing economy way — the great social equalizer and social collaborator, promoting solidarity and collaborative consumption.

The Hypercube allows you to become — concurrently and holistically — a consumer, investor and social business innovator.

Being a second or secondary home, the Hypercube can also be utilized in the following manner in so far as the "living" aspect is concerned:

- weekend retreat: getting away from the city
- guest accommodation: hosting outstation or overseas guests
- social space/ bachelor mess: organizing a private party or screening a movie
- therapeutic sanctuary: practicing alternative medicine or private meditation
- home-stay program: listing with Airbnb, etc., for income generation
- co-housing: having roommates and housemates

It is not encouraged, however, to use the Hypercube as a primary residence, even though it can be used as such, since it is meant to be a hybrid of the first (home), second (workplace) and third (social condenser) places.

Co-living

Our concept of home is shifting to the co-living movement. Also known as co-housing, the objective is to form a much desired networked community (See Chapter 6). It's worth repeating that the Hypercube is not (and should not) just be a space for living. The Hypercube allows you to become — concurrently and holistically — a consumer, investor and social business innovator, so that it is a great social equalizer and social collaborator.

Chapter 13: Work

Work defines us. We are known by way of what we do for a living. In fact, in the eyes of many, an unemployed person has no so-called "identity." He or she has no social standing and is practically cut off from the economic system prevailing in our society. This is the sorrow and tragedy of being unemployed. With the global unemployment and underemployment problem looming large in the coming decades, we have to seriously look into the future of work.

The Future of Work

Lynda Gratton examines the future of work in her excellent book, *The Shift*. In it, she mentions the choices we have to make on what we work on, how we work, where we work and with whom we work. Our quality of life depends on the choices we make and the trade-off involved. This requires our capacity to meet the three challenges she lists:

> The first is the extent to which you are able to invest in your intellectual capital over the period of your working life in order to build mastery in areas that interest you.

> The second will be the extent to which you are able to invest in your social capital through your friendships and networks. The most valuable network for you will be those that balance deep friendships with those whom you can trust and much wider networks with people who are very different to you.

The third challenge is to navigate between the old traditional work deal that had money and consumption at its heart to a working deal that has at its centre the capacity to be creative and productive and to live a life based more on experiences.

There are, therefore, three shifts, as Gratton writes in the article "The Changing Shape of Jobs: Work the Shift":

1. from shallow generalist to serial master
2. from isolated competitor to innovative connector
3. from voracious consumer to impassioned producer

This looks very much like the idea that the past is the future and we must revert back to a horticultural society — with a high-tech touch and high dose of LWTLP. This is also very similar to the concept of LEAN Logic advocated by Dr. David Fleming in his book carrying the same title.

Downshifting

Whenever we talk about an issue like an alternative work-mode and lifestyle, similar terms like "values systems and lifestyles" and "downshifting" will inevitably crop up. Slow Movement — an Australian organization that mobilizes consumers — defined "downshifting," in a blog post called "Downshifting as a Way of Life."

Who hasn't wanted to step off the ever-accelerating treadmill of work and gain some balance in life? Most of us, at one time or another, have wanted to move from the fast track of life to a more satisfying, healthier, less work-focused lifestyle.

Downshifters are people who adopt long-term voluntary simplicity in their life. They accept less money through fewer hours worked in order to have time for the important things in life. Downshifters also place emphasis on consuming less in order to reduce their ecological footprint.

There are two primary aspects to downshifting. One is about connection — connection to life, family, food and place. The other is about maintaining a healthy balance — balance in the personal, work, family, spiritual, physical and social aspects of their life ... Basically downshifters seek a life filled with more passion and purpose, meaning, fulfilment and happiness. A life to look back on with no regrets.

Downshifters want to slow down at work in order to "upshift" in others areas of their lives. For most people, the change to a slow life through downshifting comes after a long quest for true happiness and fulfilment. For others it may come after a significant life event such as severe illness, relationship breakup, bankruptcy, or the death of someone close ...

We can downshift by working fewer hours in our present job, or by accepting a job with less responsibility in the company, or we can quit our job and find another one that we find more rewarding. Or we can start our own part or full-time business, perhaps working from home.

Although we can stay where we are to downshift even if that is in the suburbs, many people do move to other locations, e.g. to the coast — seachange — or to the rural country areas — treechange.

Sometimes downshifters find they make more money, but are happier and more fulfilled — usually because they have found something that fires their passion, and work is no longer work (but "Play").

A related Slow Movement article, "Seachange-Treechange-Hillchange — a Change to Slow Movement," explains the importance of making changes like these.

Seachange has become a buzzword that has been the subject of government reports and academic studies. It seems most people would like a seachange but not all people are brave enough to make the change. And this desire for a dramatic transformation is not new. People have been escaping, or dreaming of escaping, from high-pressure metropolitan lifestyles for decades or longer. What is different now is that people in large numbers are really escaping and making the change ...

Downshifting and seachanging can be the same thing but they need not be. For example, you can downshift and stay in the city, and you can seachange and keep a high income.

The Hypercube can cause a seachange or treechange. You can escape the rat race. Start by learning more about upcoming neighborhoods and regions, lifestyle properties for sale, employment options, stories about real people, events and advice.

Half-Farmer, Half-X

Another interesting alternative (similar approach to treechange) coming from Japan highlights a similar attempt. Mr. Naoki Shiomi is the author of *Half-Farmer, Half-X (半農半X)* and founder of the Half-Farmer, Half-X Research Center in Kyoto, Japan.

"Half-farmer, half-x" is drawing much attention as a new key phrase for a lifestyle in the 21st century. "Half-farmer" refers to "a lifestyle with a touch of farming," and the "x" in "half-x" refers to an individual's profession, passion, purpose, social mission or natural calling. The synergy is enlightening to the individual's pursuit of wealth, health and happiness as he or she makes real contributions to the world.

This concept can form an excellent alliance with permaculture, an essential part of mankind's future in the coming food, fuel and financial crises.

Due to the transformational nature of the alliance of farmer and passion, those joining in the movement can be referred to as "transfarmers," transforming themselves, the land and the world.

More details on permaculture and transfarmers are available in a slide presentation here.

Combining permaculture and transfarming is also part of the Hypercube concept, advancing the wonderful initiative of "half-farmer, half-x" in other parts of the world. As the Hypercube initiative grows to non-urban areas such as rural farm lands, orchards and forests, an extended version of the Hypercube cluster forms are located locally, regionally and globally. However, even in the urban areas, the principles of permaculture (particularly the issue of sustainability and resilience) could be extensively applied even in non-agricultural settings, such as in the required sustainability or viability of any business proposal or business model.

Chapter 14: Travel

We are all familiar with various forms of tours and travels. In fact, we even differentiate conventional tour packages designed for tourists, travelers and sojourners.

Tourists are generally interested in visiting touristic spots and possibly shopping, very much like the experience of traveling in tour packages.

Travelers are more interested in the cultural aspects, covering religions, languages, cuisines, arts and handicrafts, politics and economy.

Sojourners, on the other hand, are much more progressive in their perspective. They often opt for slow travel, becoming "local residents" immersing themselves in the ways of living of the locals, very much into the deep cultural aspects. They partake in the ordinary life of the locals, observing how they work and play, learning from them and the value systems behind these activities, even doing voluntary work as a contribution back to the local society. This can be a life-changing experience.

Nomads (digital or otherwise) are yet another type of traveler engaging in long trips throughout the year, very often linked to earning an income while traveling. This is in sharp contrast to all previous types who are just "spenders or consumers" engaged in consumption and not so much in the production of incomes.

The ultimate travelers (if there is such thing) are, of course, permanent travelers or super-nomads who are constantly on the move for both production of incomes (international businesses or professions), consumption and investment. They are the "world-citizens," literally.

Reverse Travel

But what about "reverse traveling," also referred to as "inverse travel" or "flip travel"?

In its simplest terms, "reverse travel" is, of course, the reverse of travel. Instead of traveling to meet other people (understanding their culture, customs, languages, regional foods, etc.), the idea is to have these travelers come to meet you face-to-face. Reverse travel allows you to savor the many flavors of traveling without having to incur expense and time for traveling, all in the comfort of your own home.

How can you experience reverse travel? Well, it's as simple as opening up your home to travelers, backpackers and nomads. This can be done in the following ways or formats:

- home-stay program (Airbnb)
- free bed or couch accommodation (Couchsurfing)
- free tour guide (FreeTour.com)
- home exchange (HomeExchange)
- house sitters/caretakers (House Sitting Worldwide)
- warm showers and/or accommodation for cyclists (Warm Showers)
- meal sharing (Meal Sharing)
- volunteer programs (Helpx)

The property at home acts as a base for you to host travelers. You travel passively because travelers come and stay with you, with all their exciting traveling tales. When you later decide to travel actively, you have the option to be hosted (reciprocally by travelers you have hosted earlier while in "reverse mode") anywhere around the world, because of your "reverse travel" contributions. What a wonderful world of traveling!

In order to properly play host to overseas travelers, you might want to have adequate space (although any space could serve the purpose). The Hypercube could be an excellent vehicle for such a purpose. You will be building your own social safety net via the shared ownership of property and a social network while traveling worldwide for life.

Chapter 15: Learn

Neuroscientist Sebastian Seung maps a new model of the brain in his TED Talk, presenting the connections between each neuron — which he refers to as our "connectome." It's as individual as our genome. In other words, your connectomes determine your character and personality, just like your genetic makeup defines your being.

Presumably, we could improve our being by having more connections (neuron or otherwise) via the following methods:

- lifelong learning
- frequent brainstorming sessions
- deep meditation
- networking (social or professional)

Thus the connectomes could be of three types, one acting through our body (genes or our DNA or genome), one acting through our mind (memes or memories or cultural imprint), one acting through our spirit (what I would call "zenes", or a Zen-like meditation practice, including karmic acts and social "networking", etc.). Therefore, the body-mind-spirit is equivalent to gene-meme-zene, which can actually give a more illuminating picture of what is happening when we say our well-being is conditioned by our body-mind-spirit. It is the action and reaction of our gene-meme-zene. You are your gene-meme-zene.

We could then have a perfect theory for human behavior, captured in just three words: gene, meme and zene.

GDP vs. True Well-Being

The most-often-used measure of a country's well-being is the gross domestic product, or GDP, but it fails to properly measure the well-being and happiness of its citizens. Therefore, there are many alternative measures proposed to do a better job, such as the genuine progress indicator, gross national happiness index, happy planet index, and social progress index.

In a very similar fashion, many current measures of financial returns are not able to measure the true prosperity of individuals. They are concerned with returns on investment (ROI) rather than returns on life (ROL), missing the very essential elements that make life fulfilling and meaningful.

Life Portfolio or Portfolio Life?

To put it in yet another way: Don't just go for a life portfolio (things such as jobs, assets, investments, businesses or other résumé virtues); go for a portfolio life (experiences such as community, travel, play, spiritual and other virtues).

Or as they say: "Buy experience, not things," "better, not more" and "develop, not grow."

However, the Hypercube initiative is designed to achieve both: "Own it. Live it." With the Hypercube, you can have things (a second home) *and* experience, get better *and* more (social franchise), grow *and* develop (the commons). It is both having a life portfolio (the Hypercube clusters — see chapter 7) and a portfolio life (LWTLP). It yields both résumé virtues and eulogy virtues at the same time.

Chapter 16: Play

The word "play" has two distinctive meanings — one narrow and one broad. In its narrow sense, it means entertainment and relaxation or recreation. In its broad sense, it means "passion converts work and life into play."

Work is generally left-brain related, rational and analytical — the heritage of the enlightenment approach. Life should be, on the other hand, fun, playful and very much right-brain-related. It is the enlivenment (or enlightenment 2.0) perspective that leads to the economy of the commons, providing "healthy ecosystems, economic security, stronger communities and a participatory culture," according to Commons Rising, a report by the Tomales Bay Institute. Then we can realize objective benefits and experience subjective pleasure and joy.

The earth would be a much better place if we worked with our left-brain, lived with our right-brain and shared the commons, according Andreas Weber's 2013 essay, "Enlivenment: Towards a Fundamental Shift in the Concepts of Nature, Culture and Politics":

> Unlike market economics, commoning is not only about producing and distributing resources; it's also about constructing meaningful relationships to a place, to the Earth and to one another. The shift from a neo-Darwinian/ neo-Liberal economy to a world of biospheric householding is not a utopian dream ... Being an active participant in the biosphere does not mean to "obey all its laws," but to enact freedom within the constraints of existential and ecological necessity ... For the German philosopher and poet Friedrich Schiller the paradox of equally fulfilling our need

to belong and our need to be autonomous is the culmination point of culture. In his concept of "aesthetic education" Schiller expressed his conviction that a negotiation of these paradoxes was necessary to live a true and meaningful life, a life that fulfils its potential and at the same time reveals the aliveness of the larger whole, and in this sense is aesthetic or poetic ... For Schiller, the entanglement of individual autonomy and larger necessity could only – momentarily – be fulfilled through play. Play unfolds from a person's free choice about how to do what is necessary, and this opens up new possibilities in the process. We are fully human only in play, Schiller believed. We are natural only in play, one might add. It is not entirely fanciful to suggest that the practice of an enlivened economy amounts to nothing less than the practice of a rich and playful life. That vision, the deep attraction and satisfaction of serious play, may be the most potent, imaginative force for helping us deal with the realities of our time.

Or, as psychologist Marshall Rosenberg expressed in his book *The Heart of Social Change*, "Don't do anything that isn't play." If we are meeting our own needs, it will be play, and our own needs are in constant transformation, entangled in a continuous material and meaningful world hitched to everything else.

"Play" could be considered the "sweet spot" of the Hypercube initiative, as the ultimate purpose is to achieve a state of flow or ecstasy. The freedom, fun and fulfillment we experience is the result of the convergence of living, working, traveling and learning in our daily lives. Life is then free, active and meaningful—"delightful Play".

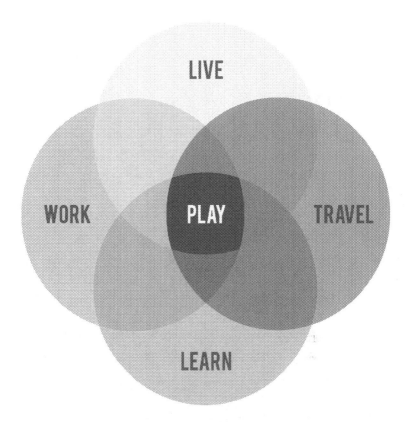

The Hypercube initiative is designed to bring about the convergence, interaction and interdependence of the live, work, travel and learn elements to yield the "play" moment – either individually or in different combinations – when we make the best and full use of the personal space created.

Chapter 17: Experience & Transformation

The evolution of the economy of the world has gone through the following stages:

1. Agrarian
2. Industrial
3. Service
4. Experience
5. Transformation

The first stage involved agriculture, farming and other extractive activities such as mining. The key attribute is fungible and natural.

The second stage involved industries engaged with the making of things. The key attribute is tangible and standardized.

The third stage involved sectors that deliver services on demand, which are customized and intangible.

The fourth stage involved the creation of a "stage" that provided memorable personal experiences revealed over a duration of time.

The fifth stage involved the provision of guidance for the effectual transformation of the individual so elicited and sustained through time.

The Hypercube initiative is to provide an experiential and transformational setting (both in hardware and software) that will bring forth the much needed changes in our global mentality and subconscious minds for a successful transition to the new sharing economy.

Chapter 18: Life Transcendence and Life TranscenDANCE

When we examine life in general, we can quickly realize that it's a business. It is a business of living, surviving and prospering. It has the characteristics of sustainability, just like a business entity.

Life is also a personal business — a business of managing scarce resources (including time), social relationships, issues of health (including stress) and information. The application of business management tools (covering hardware and software) is not only relevant but also essential.

People talk a lot about investment portfolios, but few are aware of portfolio life (a diverse lifestyle covering LWTLP). We think our investment portfolio will give us happiness and freedom, which may not often be the case. We can actually find more fun, fulfillment and meaning in our portfolio life (LWTLP) rather than in our life portfolio (what we own and possess, just like our investment portfolios accumulated through life).

So, what is a portfolio life? A portfolio life is a strategic plan of action and orientation to life — a perspective that spans today's goals and tomorrow's legacies. It represents your work, your interests and what you have done. It represents who you are.

Like a successful investment portfolio, a portfolio life has diverse components, such as LWTLP. With a suitable, viable, and sustainable combination of LWTLP, an ideal portfolio life will be attained for each individual.

Résumé Virtues or Eulogy Virtues?

In 2014, David Brooks, columnist for The New York Times, delivered a TED Talk about human virtues.

The résumé virtues are the ones you put on your résumé, which are the skills you bring to the marketplace. The eulogy virtues are the ones that get mentioned in the eulogy, which are deeper: who are you in your depth, what is the nature of your relationships, are you bold, loving, dependable, do you have consistency, etc.

Very often, these two sides of our nature are at war with each other. We live in perpetual self-confrontation between external success and internal value. And the tricky thing, I'd say, about these two sides of our nature is they work by different logics. The external logic is an economic logic: input leads to output, risk leads to reward. The internal side of our nature is a moral logic and often an inverse logic. You have to give to receive. You have to surrender to something outside yourself to gain strength within yourself. You have to conquer the desire to get what you want. In order to fulfill yourself, you have to forget yourself. In order to find yourself, you have to lose yourself.

The cost of being a specialist, someone living by résumé virtues, is that we often forgo the benefits of being a generalist and living by eulogy virtues. A generalist nurtures the many sides of who we are, using a multiplicity of talents and incorporating LWTLP elements. We have a chance to shape our work to suit the way we live instead of shaping our lives to fit our work.

Transcendence

Of course, there is always the even bigger picture. When we transcend the life portfolio, we receive the wisdom of seeing the integrated whole, the unity and the interconnection of all things and all beings. Simply put, transcendence is very similar to the gradual progress from SOHO-1 to SOHO-2 and SOHO-3, as pointed out in the evolution of the SOHO taxonomy. According to Dr. Lars Tornstam, author of *Gerotranscendence: A Developemental Theory of Positive Aging*, transcendence involves "a shift in meta-perspective — from a materialistic and rational perspective to a more cosmic and transcendent one."

This is progress toward wisdom, scaling from local to global and then cosmic. A transcendent individual experiences, Tornstam writes, "a new understanding of fundamental existential questions." He or she often feels a "cosmic communion with the spirit of the universe, a redefinition of time, space, life and death" and a "redefinition of the self and relationships to others."

"The individual becomes, for example, less self-occupied and at the same time more selective in the choice of social and other activities. There is an increased feeling of affinity with past generations and a decreased interest in superfluous social interaction," according to Tornstam. Connection to a networked community, as envisaged in the Hypercube initiative, requires social interaction and makes it essential.

This state of transcendent being is a cause for celebration. It's a dance of transcendence or "transcendance," a term first used by Joan M. Erikson in the extended version of the book, *The Life Cycle Completed*, co-authored by Erik H. Erikson.

The Hypercube is an experimentation of this transcendance. It's the element of "play" in the overall scheme of things (see Chapter 16: Play)

Chapter 19: Hypercube as a Living Experiment for Systems Thinking

According to Dr. Kathia Laszlo, author and life coach, a system is a set of interconnected elements that form a whole. The elements show properties of the whole rather than of the individual elements.

My interpretation: "From Systems Thinking to Systems Feeling to Systems Being to Systems Living"

In her presentation on systems thinking, she references Peter Checkland's book *Systems Thinking, Systems Practice*. In it, he defines "systems thinking" as thinking about the world as a "system." Systems thinking requires looking at processes rather than structures, relationships rather than components, and interconnections rather than separations.

Systems thinking takes analysis – answering the "what" and "how" questions – and synthesis – answering the "why" and "what for" questions – and combines them. "By combining analysis and synthesis," Laszlo says, "systems thinking creates a rich inquiring platform."

The unity, interconnectedness and relatedness of a system can cause strong emotions the first time we realize or see it, Laszlo says. Astronaut Rusty Schweickart illustrated the impact of systems thinking after seeing Earth from space. Schweickart's first look at our planet created in him a new way of viewing systems as a whole. This is systems feeling:

> From the moon, the Earth is so small and so fragile, and such a precious little spot in that Universe, that you

can block it out with your thumb. Then you realize that on that spot, that little blue and white thing, is everything that means anything to you – all of history and music and poetry and art and death and birth and love, tears, joy, games, all of it right there on that little spot that you can cover with your thumb. And you realize from that perspective that you've changed forever, that there is something new there, that the relationship is no longer what it was.

Systems being (being aware of belonging to the "whole") and systems living (living a lifestyle that supports the integrity of the system) work together to link head, heart and hands, Laszlo says. "The expression of systems being is an integration of our full human capacity. It involves rationality with reverence to the mystery of life, listening beyond words, sensing with our whole being, and expressing our authentic self in every moment of our life. The journey from systems thinking to systems being is a transformative learning process of expansion of consciousness — from awareness to embodiment," she says.

The Hypercube and Systems Living

The Hypercube initiative is a living experimentation of systems thinking, systems feeling, systems being and systems living or kind of Ethical Design as promoted by Aral and his team of ind.ie.

The systems thinking behind the Hypercube project can be gleaned from the SOHO taxonomy. SOHO-1 (small office/ home office) represents the *local* quality of work, SOHO-2 (Solar Heliospheric Observatory) represents the *global* quality of living, SOHO-3 (self-organizing holarchical open system) represents the *cosmic* quality of life, and SOHO-4 (sociable home) represents the physical construct and the integration of the local-global-cosmic perspective that leads to holistic well-being, happiness and meaningfulness.

This feeling of holistic well-being, happiness and meaningfulness is the systems feeling. It's the play and flow moment and the very "sweet spot" that we are all pursuing all our life.

From that moment on, we become a systems being, fully aware and appreciative of belonging to the whole. We become truly and fully human.

To continue to have this wonderful feeling, we only have to do one thing: our daily lifestyle should be systems living, living a lifestyle that supports and sustains the very systems that we are a part of (rather than living apart from them).

This is, of course, very similar to living a lifestyle that integrates our body, mind and spirit. Why and how is this so? We could again trace the systemic connections, or connectomes — a term popularized in the study of the brain and mind.

The connectomes could be of three types: one acting through our body (DNA, genome, or genes), one acting through our mind (memories, cultural imprint, or memes), and one acting through our spirit (meditation, like Zen practice, including karmic acts and social networking, or zenes). Therefore, the body, mind and spirit is equivalent to the gene, meme and zene, which can actually give a more illuminating picture of what is happening when we say our well-being is conditioned by our body, mind and spirit. It is the action and reaction of our gene, meme and zene. You are your gene, meme and zene systems.

We could then possibly have a perfect systemic theory for human behavior, captured in just three words: gene, meme and zene.

Therefore, through the SOHO taxonomy, the Hypercube initiative brings about the systemic integration of the local, global and cosmic as well as the body, mind and spirit into our daily lives via the elements of live, work, travel, learn, play. This attempt is also similar to the Ethical Design promoted by Aral and his team at ind.ie (see Appendix J

Chapter 20: Own It. Live It. Spread it.

Investment in property is vital for our financial security and well-being, and there are many ways we can do it:

- direct individual investment
- property investment holding companies
- cooperative societies or unions
- real estate investment trust (REIT)
- The Hypercube initiative

What is the main difference between the Hypercube initiative and all the others? It is the essential combination of owning it and living it.

All the other forms of property investment involve direct or indirect ownership. But they all lack the element of *living* in the truest sense of the word. They lack the holistic lifestyle of live, work, travel, learn, and play— which is so essential for our own well-being. It's how we find meaning, happiness and freedom in a connected community.

It is this combination of means (way or mechanism), modes (the physical form) and meanings (purpose or why) that makes the Hypercube initiative unique.

The networked community is crucial to the commons. It is this practice of the commons and commoning that brings a totally different perspective to our life, particularly in view of the emergence of alternative socio-economic systems replacing the prevailing paradigms (capitalism, socialism or communism).

Only the Hypercube initiative provides this "Own it. Live it. Spread it" advantage as well as the relevant ecosystem and facilities to enjoy it. It acts effectively as a transition to a new world where the triple bottom lines of profit, people and planet, or economy, equity and environment are at the core.

Own it. Live it. Spread it.

Owning is simple

- Plan A: Buy (property ownership)
- Plan B: Rent (home-sharing)
- Plan C: Commons (combination: Sharing Economy)

Living is holistic:

- Live (Second Home for 2nd Life for Millennials and 3rd Agers)
- Work (Business incubator / Accelerator /LEAN Startup)
- Travel (Holiday exchange / Reverse Travel)
- Learn (Life-Long-Learning or LQ- Learning Quotient)
- Play (Freedom. Passion. Vision)

Spreading it is missionary:

- "1+3 Plan" (Climbing the property ladder)
- Social Business (overcoming inequality in property ownership)
- Activism in The Commons (Sharing & Solidarity Economy)

Chapter 21:The Third Choice: Rich, Poor or Hypercube

When we talk about money, there are two approaches, according to Japanese writer Ken Honda, in his book *Eight Steps to Happiness & Prosperity* (original edition in Japanese).

The knowledge or skills connected with money acquisition is the so-called "money IQ" (intelligence quotient), while our values systems, emotional attachment or relationship to money is the so-called "money EQ" (emotion quotient).

A person with a high money IQ would likely be rich or super-rich. A person with a low money IQ would likely be poor. A person with a high money EQ would likely hold positive value systems (so-called "happy and contended"). A person with a low money EQ would hold negative value systems (so-called "unhappy and dissatisfied"). Therefore a person with a good balance of money IQ and money EQ would likely be both rich and happy, which is certainly a rare combination.

However, if a rich person doesn't necessarily have a high money EQ, that person will lead a miserable life, in spite (or even because) of the accumulated wealth, due to the wrong priority value systems.

On the other hand, a happy and content person may not necessarily have a high money IQ, lacking the knowledge and skills (maybe even the intention, motivation and will) to acquire or own earthly wealth, which may result in the need for social support systems or a social security net.

Life is a journey of choice. Sometimes, you can choose to be rich. Not making such a choice is also a choice — the default choice being poor, unhappy and dissatisfied due to lack of action.

However, there is now a third choice available. You can choose to be neither rich nor poor. You can choose to be a "Hypercuber," someone who owns (or more correctly, shares the ownership of) a Hypercube and lives a Hypercube way of life. It is the "Own it. Live it" choice. It is having a high money IQ and high money EQ at the same time.

You are invited to be actively involved in this social movement towards having both a money IQ and a money EQ as well as exploring the related means, modes and meanings of the Hypercube initiative (see also Appendix L:

Chapter 22: Conclusion

For the past many years, I have lived, experienced and studied the business sector and the social sector, a world divided into profit and nonprofit. I believe we have a golden opportunity to combine business with social concerns. Our future lies in the middle ground... This is the Third Choice.

How? By making use of a global movement called the sharing economy. It allows us to "do good, make money, and have fun."

For example, I own a valuable space that I share with others to live, work, travel, learn and play. I call it Hypercube @ SOHOland.

By living this way, I have to date met over 600 people (who have visited me and lived-in my Hypercube by private invitation) from all over the world. In a way it can be called "reverse travel" (I stay home, and travelers come to me), reaping the benefits of travel and sharing. My space is perhaps the most "sociable home" in Malaysia (or even the world). It has been social, fun and profitable for me.... A Social Business (see Appendix I for more details).

Are you looking for a way to own a property and grow it into a chain or cluster of properties? I would love to have 15-minute Skype session with you to explain the concept of "How to Build Your Future by Starting a Social Business." (See also Appendix K

To get a link to book a 15-minute session on Skype or a scheduled webinar, send me an email at ericolot1300@ gmail.com.

Recent Blog Postings

(1)Blog Post dated 4th January 2018:

New Year Wish 2018

On 31st December 2012 (a solid 5 years ago), I listed my New Year Wish which is reproduced below (kind of deja vu)?!

All I really needed is a second home,
where I can house my friends over-night whenever I need to,
where I can have my own lean business startup with full business centre facilities,
where I can collaborate with other micro-entrepreneurs and mentors,
where I can play host to couchsurfers / vacationers from all over the world,
where I can organize work-shop to exchange skills,
where I can have karaoke sessions with my friends,
where I can preview movies in home comfort,
where I can have Ogawa therapeutic massage whenever I want,
where I can meet my Mastermind Group members, planning the next second homes

All I really needed is a second home,
which is seller-financed with zero down and zero interest,
which is leased with option to purchase,
which is held as Realshares deemed better than REITs,
which is self-financing and sustainable,
which could be bequeathed to my future generations,

All I really needed is a second home,
that advocates and practices the Triple-Bottom-Line (3Ps),
that yields Profit,
that connects People,
that takes care of the Planet,
that captures the spirit of Collaborative Consumption,
that includes Peer2Peer, Share Economy, Freeconomy, Gift-Economy
and Open Source etc.

What is the latest status now?

Well.... I am still running / pivoting the project over the 5-year period and subsequent. Luckily the condominium unit was acquired in cash, so there is very little cash outlay over the period, with costs more than covered with incomes from Airbnb, short-terms leases and co-working spaces, training courses and tour-programs etc.

The biggest "achievement" has been the social interactions with more than 500-plus guests from the hosting of couch-surfers / workcationers / volunteers. I enjoyed very much such "reverse travels" (I stay home, travelers come to see me). This is one of the best ways to spend time for retirees and other similarly inclined. Through such contacts, the project had also been highlighted in Ukrainian TV (novy. tv) and some travel journal video, not to mention my own local productions: (1) Jungle Trekking at AhPek / Saga Hill, Cheras) (2) Hot-spring at Jalan Sg. Lallang, Semenyih) (3) Karaoke Session at Hypercube@SOHOLand,Cheras.

Due to the relatively new concept introduced, the awareness / understanding of the project by the public is still low and a lot of education / promotion would obviously be required. The urgent task is to introduce an easily understood equivalent. I have a feeling that idea of a "Bitcoin" equivalent could be very useful, particularly in view of the publicity generated by Bitcoin based on Blockchain technology.

My next "pivoting" of the project should be in the direction of "Tokenization" of the project, possibly via an ICO (Initial Coin Offering"):

This shall be my New Year Wish 2018 (a deja vu?!): A Second Home for Everyone. In some way it is a Re-Solution from 2012?!

LEAN PROPERTY (精益房產) is an Eco-System

PROPERTY CHAINS
via
BLOCKCHAIN

Your consumption (as user of the property) can be skillfully turned into your production / business / investment (as a Lean Startup (精益創業) business and property chain ownership) and much more (such as health, wealth and happiness) in the near future.

This is made possible by the project's eco-system.

(2)Blog Post dated 2nd Jan 2018:

Why the New Year 2018 is Auspicious Year

The New Year 2018 is definitely going to be an interesting and wholistic one, because the countdown to the New Year 2018 was done in the clear sky of Full Moon which is most auspicious. I was personally first time aware of such a cosmic event and had personally experienced this in the most prominent land-mark in Malaysia… the Petronas Twin Tower!

The Countdown to Year 2018 at the Petronas Twin Tower was most boisterous I had ever experienced, in the company of two couch-surfers from Iran (another first for me), Nastran and her brother Amir....

The New Year 2018 Countdown:

(3) Blog Post dated: 4th March 2017

Don't be a Dirty Old Man

Don't Be a Dirty Old Man (Dipper/Dropper)

* *Traditional Retirement: Don't be a "Dipper / Dropper" (Ungentlemanly). Be a "Upper / Flipper" (Gentlemanly)*
* *Work Extension*
* *New Vision in Retirement Planning*
* *Legacy*

This is the direct or literal translation of the titles (in Chinese) of these two books translated from Japanese whose authors have caused quite a social storm in Japan.

The content is definitely NOT what you might think (sexual connotations), taking hints from the titles (shame on you)! In fact, it is about something much more important in our individual life and life journey, in the context of mobility or flow (upwardly or downwardly) of the aging population: Money, Perspective on Money, Aging and Retirement, Health, Wealth and Happiness. Think of the buzzword "Yuppies", if you want to get into the right context, mood or perspective.

The Dirty Old Man refers to the Downwardly Mobile Aged Person (a Dipper or Dropper), while the Gentlemanly Old Man refers to the Upwardly Mobile Aged Person (an Upper or Flipper). Dippers / Droppers are experiencing substantial reduction in income / purchasing power. The Uppers / Flippers are inventing ways to reduce the impact of reduction of income / purchasing power, by paying more attention to alternative economic models such as collaborative consumption / sharing economy and the emphasis on non-monetary needs such as intellectual and emotional or spiritual concerns.

The social issue of fast growing number of Dippers / Droppers is causing grave concern in Japan and many developed and developing countries. The possible solution points to the direction of creating more Uppers / Flippers amongst the aged in particular, and over-all population in general.

This is also an excellent way to introduce Aging Literacy, an issue or education that will affect everyone, either now (e.g. having aging parents) or in the near future (we are all getting old)!

The message is then clear: Don't be a Dirty Old Man. Be a Gentlemanly Old Man. Be an Upper / Flipper NOT a Dipper / Dropper! Do think of your aging parents NOW if you are still so blessed.... and prepare yourself for the soon-arriving event (your own Retirement)!

Earlier Related Blog Posts

- *Inconspicuous Consumption (28/12/17)*

- *Experiencing NATURE / CULTURE / NURTURE in Kuala Lumpur (21/9/17)*

- *How To Save the World and Humanity (13/9/17)*

Inconspicuous Consumption

We all heard of "Conspicuous Consumption" (the use of particular goods through which the status is revealed e.g. luxurious cars)....there is now a brand new phrase known as "Inconspicuous Consumption" (status through prizing knowledge and building cultural capital), signifying a shift in values system or trans-valuation, resulting in a new elite class different from the leisure class, called "aspirational class" by Elizabeth Currid-Halkett in her new book "The Sum of Small Things: A Theory of the Aspirational Class".

"More profoundly, investment in education, healthcare and retirement has a notable impact on consumers' quality of life, and also on the future life chances of the next generation. Today's inconspicuous consumption is a far more pernicious form of status spending than the conspicuous consumption of Veblen's time. Inconspicuous consumption – whether breastfeeding or education – is a means to a better quality of life and improved social mobility for one's own children, whereas conspicuous consumption is merely an end in itself – simply ostentation. For today's aspirational class, inconspicuous consumption choices secure and preserve social status, even if they do not necessarily display it."

I have some hilarious personal experience with such Inconspicuous Consumption. Over the years, I have been hosting hundreds of backpackers from all over the world via a web-site called "Couch-Surfing" (www.couchsurfing.com). By hosting such travelers using my spare room or even couch in the lounge, I have been perceived to be rich and influential in my neighborhood, even though I do not display any ostentation of outward wealth (which I do not really need). I thoroughly enjoyed the experience, interacting with people from diverse background in culture, age and racial composition etc., greatly enhancing my "quality of life" in retirement and health, in addition to able to do "Life-Long-Learning" PLUS always having beautiful birds as company! I thus become unknowingly the "Aspirational Class", the new elite, prizing knowledge and building cultural capital.

In fact, such Inconspicuous Consumption can form the basis for a paradigm shift in social equality by shifting emphasis from material consumption to immaterial consumption----- a typical case of "Skilling-up" (acquiring new skills) and "Powering Down" (cutting down material and energy consumption), something the world urgently need to do.

The required skilling up obviously has to enable us to tackle the expected hardship brought about by the convergence of many crises such as fuel, food and finance etc. The essence is toward self-sufficiency, sustainability and voluntary simplicity.

The solution places heavy demand for new skill-sets (Skill-up) and lifestyle changes (Power-down), covering the physical, financial, emotional, social, intellectual and spiritual aspects of our life. This sounds like a wholistic approach….. such as many intentional communities or eco-villages practicing Permaculture.

Back to the case of my personal experience: Climbing your Property Ladder is not just for house ownership. In our context, House should not be treated as a mere Noun. It should be a powerful Verb….. carrying out meaningful and impactful activities, using the house as a combination of First Place / Second Place / Third Place as defined by American urban sociologist Professor Ray

Oldenburg: First Place (Home), Second Place (Place-of-work), Third Place (Place for Social Optimization): http://bit.ly/2iC84Wl so you will have the Most Powerful Personal Space (5-fold better than any BMW, Benz?!) in your locality, whether locally, regionally or globally.

This is truly a shining example of Inconspicuous Consumption.... skilling up and powering down.

References:

1. https://www.theatlantic.com/magazine/archive/2008/07/inconspicuous-consumption/306845/
2. http://www.economist.com/node/5323772
3. https://www.huffingtonpost.com/perry-garfinkel/the-7-laws-of-inconspicuo_b_381954.html

Experiencing NATURE / CULTURE / NURTURE

Short-Stay / Long-Stay Tour-Experience

Nature / Culture / Nurture
- *Forest Bath near Kuala Lumpur (Nature)*
- *10,000 steps in Kuala Lumpur (Culture)*
- *3rd Ager Lifestyle & Digital Nomad 2nd Life (Nurture)*
- Exploring (FREE): Sharing Economy / Lean Logic / Minimalism
- Opportunity to meet or become Local Guru

Experience NATURE / CULTURE / NURTURE / using the principles in LEAN LOGIC (by Dr. David Fleming). Walk through with us the exciting Short-stay / Long-stay tour activities and the 3rd Ager Lifestyle, possibly the least known / prepared yet longest period in your life! We need to nurture such environment and ecosystem.

Local Tours & Attractions:

- Forest Bath near Kuala Lumpur (Nature)

- 10,000 Steps in Kuala Lumpur (Culture)
- 3rd Ager Lifestyle (Nurture)

  FREE exposition on Life Course: Sharing Economy/Lean Logic/Minimalist (Nurture)

- 1st Ager: 1-20 (growing up & receiving education)
- 2nd Ager: 21-55 (earning a living & raising a family)
- 3rd Ager: 56 and beyond (Second Life after "graduating" from Career), possibly the least known / least prepared, yet longest period in your Life.

You are never too young or too old to live the 3rd Ager Lifestyle: NOW is the time to nurture such environment / ecosystem.

Please come and join us this coming Saturday (23/9/17) **http://bit. ly/2wEhtCt** (and subsequent weeks, with varying topics on the same theme on Nature / Culture / Nurture), we will be having a lively presentation and discussion on NATURE / CULTURE / NURTURE, and related issues such as working prototypes / projects / proposals etc., by virtue of being or becoming LEAN!

This is also your opportunity to meet or become a LOCAL GURU.

How to Save the World
and Humanity

Which One Will Save the World & Humanity?!

The Warp Drive (EM Drive)
* Propellantless Propulsion system that can reach Mars in weeks.
* High-tech for space travel.

TLUD (Top-Lit Updraft Kiln)
* A portable Kiln that makes biochar from organic wastes.
* Low-tech: Carbon-negative fuel and soil enrichments.

I saw two extreme posts / articles on Facebook this morning. The contrast was so dramatic that I have to write something on this observation.

The Warp Drive (EM Drive) is currently being developed by the NASA and the Chinese who is rumored to have successfully tested the device. It is a propullentless propulsion system (against the physical law as is generally known) that can send man to Mars in weeks.... a kind of must-have for man's exploration / conquest of outer space.

The other device is extremely down-to-earth and low-tech. It is called TLUD (Top-Lit Updraft) Kiln or burner that uses organic wastes to generate heat AND produces bio-char (biological charcoal) that has been proven to be an excellent additive for soil enrichment. It is also possibly the only carbon-negative way of heating, through partial combustion (pyrolysis). The whole process therefore locks-in carbon-dioxide from the air (through photosynthesis by plants as organic wastes) in the form of bio-char.... an excellent way to control global warming.

Will humanity's future depends on our ability to "migrate" to Mars (possibly via Warp Drive) or other planets? OR alternatively embrace Mother Earth with a new version of Ecological Civilization..... Why not BOTH, indeed?!

OR is there a Third Way? The Third Choice.......http://bit. ly/2h2rx2i

Index

APPLE 2.0: p.35

Author: p.99

Baby Boomer: p. xi

Biochar: p.34

Blockchain: p.24, 74

COCO: p.8

COHO: p.8

Co-Living / Co-Working: p.2, 11, 20, 21, 23

Collaboration: p.37

Commons: p. ix, 8-11, 14-18, 25-29

Couch-surfing: p. 82, 111, 117

COWO: p. 8

Ethical Design: p.63, 65, 123, 124, 128

Eulogy Virtue: p. 54, 60

First Place: p. 1, 9, 84, 85, 119

Gene: p. 53, 64

Great Good Place: p. 7, 9

HelpX: p. 100, 117

Hypercube: p. ix, 1-6, 23, 27, 32

IBM 2.0: p. 34

ICO: p. ix, 74

ICT: p. 34, 40

ICT 2.0: p. 34

Internship: p. 107

LEAN Logic: p. 46, 123, 127, 128

LEAN Property: p. 2, 4, 13, 124-125

LEAN Startup: p. 5, 22, 67

Life Portfolio: p. 54, 59, 61, 109

Localization: p. 6, 26, 27, 35, 41
LWTLP: p. 3, 5, 11-12, 24, 28, 38, 40, 46, 54, 59
Meme: p. 53, 64
Mentoring: p. 37, 99, 115-117
Millennials: p. xii, 2, 24, 67
MOHO: p. 8
Money IQ: p. 68, 69
Money EQ: p. 68, 69
Nomad: p. 5, 11, 50, 51, 111
Permaculture: p. 6, 26, 29, 35-36, 41, 49, 84
Place-making: p. 7, 9
Portfolio Life: p. 54, 59, 109
Resume Virtue: p. 54, 60
Reverse Travel: p. 51, 67, 70, 72
Second Place: p. 1, 7, 84-85
Seachange: p. 47, 48
Sharing Economy: p. ix, xi, 5, 12, 14, 17, 23, 70, 88, 99, 113
Social Condenser: p. xi, 44
Social Business: p. xi, 11, 17, 22, 43-44, 67, 70
SOHO1: p. 41, 42, 119
SOHO2: p. 41, 42, 119
SOHO3: p. 42, 119
SOHO4: p. 42, 119
Solidarity Economy: p. xi, xii, 5, 11, 67
SoLoMo: p. 40
SOMO: p. 41
Student Accommodation: p. 2
Systems: p. xi, 29, 31-36, 46, 50, 62-64, 68
Third Ager: p. 24, 33
Third Place: p. 1-3, 7-9, 84, 116, 119
Third Choice: p. xii, 14, 68-70, 92, 119, 121
TranscenDANCE: p. 59, 61

Transfarmer: p. 49

Transformation: p. 6, 32, 48, 56, 58

Transition: p. ix, 12, 27, 32, 34, 42, 58, 67

Treechange: p. 47, 48

Trinity: p. 123

Triple Bottom Line: p. 5, 6, 17-18, 40, 67, 121

Volunteering: p. 107

Zene: p. 53, 64

半農半X: p. 48

精益房產: p. 125

精益創業: p. 125

Appendix A

Supplementary Reading / Resources

Please refer to website; slideshare.com for further details about:

- The Convergence of Crises: the Apocalypse
- Trending towards the Managed Commons
- Business Landscape: A Comparison of Existing and Emergent Business Models
- The Holon: Independence and Interdependence
- Participation in Hypercube @ SOHOland: Mechanism & Flow
- Indicative Return on Investment (ROI)
- Live A Day Differently (LADD) Workshop

Appendix B

Author & Editor

Eric Y.F. Lim, Author

Prior to his retirement, Eric worked many years with a number of public-listed companies in the property development industry in various capacities in Malaysia, Singapore, Vietnam and most recently China. The various projects involved residential, commercial, industrial, hoteling and tourism sectors. The experience and expertise acquired enabled Eric to formulate the sociable home (SOHO)/Hypercube concept and its related SOHO technology: a holistic approach to integration of local, global and cosmic perspectives, effectively turning houses to homes to community, yielding a "great good place."

In addition, Eric is also actively involved with Airbnb (as a homestay host), Couchsurfing (as a host), training and workshops (particularly in property investments, digital literacies and life-long learning), the sharing economy and the development of the commons. These constitute the major components of the proposed program.

Being an entrepreneur himself, Eric has been doing extensive research on various aspects of information and communications technology and mobile technology, business incubators, mentoring and other corporate matters. However, he is convinced that the world is trending towards the widespread adoption of the networked commons to solve many socio-economic-environmental-political issues, hence the importance of digital literacies and life-long learning.

Amy Steele, Editor

Amy has been an editor and technical writer for the past decade. She's worked in industries such as advertising, public relations, publishing and technical specifications in the U.S. and abroad. Prior to editing *Third Choice: Rich, Poor or Commons*, she spent two and a half years teaching English in South Korea. She continues to copyedit and occasionally write for a South Korean expat magazine.

Amy and Eric met through HelpX, a volunteer exchange website that connects traveling volunteers with hosts who need an extra set of hands. Like most HelpX hosts, the Hypercube @ SOHOland accepts volunteers, who are offered accommodation and meals in exchange for work on various projects (See **Appendix D**).

Appendix C

News and perspectives on the Commons
By David Bollier

Making Networked Sharing Socially Beneficial, Not Just Predatory and Profitable

Mon, 01/11/2016 - 17:29

Every time Uber, the Web-based taxi intermediary, enters a new city, it provokes controversy about its race-to-the-bottom business practices and bullying of regulators and politicians. The problem with Uber and other network-based intermediaries such as Lyft, Task Rabbit, Mechanical Turk and others, is that they are trying to introduce brave new market structures as a *fait accompli.* They have only secondary interest in acceptable pay rates, labor standards, *consumer protections, civic and environmental impacts or democratic debate itself.*

Rather than cede these choices to self-selected venture capitalists and profit-focused entrepreneurs, some European cities and regional governments came up with a brilliant idea: devise an upfront, before-the-fact policy framework for dealing with the disruptions of the "sharing economy."

If we can agree in advance about what constitutes a socially respectful marketplace – and what constitutes a predatory free-riding on the commonweal – we'll all be a lot better off. Consumers, workers and a community will have certain basic protections. Investors and executives won't be able to complain about "unlevel playing fields" or unfair regulation. And public debate won't be a money-fueled free-for-all, but a more thoughtful, rational deliberation.

Now, if only the European Union will listen to the Committee of the Regions (CoR)! The CoR is an official assembly of regional presidents, mayors and elected representatives from 28 EU countries. It routinely expresses its views on all sorts of major policy issues that may have local or regional impacts. In December, the CoR submitted a formal statement about the "sharing economy" to the EU in an opinion written by rapporteur Benedetta Brighenti, the deputy mayor of the municipality of Castelnuovo Rangone, in the province of Modena, Italy.

Other states, provinces and cities of the world would do well to emulate this impressive, forward-looking policy statement. Entitled, "The Local and Regional Dimension of the Sharing Economy," the CoR statement sets forth a broad policy framework for dealing with the social and civic impacts of network platforms that enable new sorts of micro-rentals and piecemeal work. These are the business models most often associated with Uber, Airbnb, Task Rabbit and other "gig economy" ventures.

> *The CoR statement is remarkable, first, for proposing some worthwhile distinctions in how we think about the "sharing economy." It argues that there are really four types of economies –*
> *the "access economy" that is renting things rather than selling them permanently;*
> *the "gig economy" that hosts contingent work in digital marketplaces;*
> *the "collaborative economy" that fosters peer-to-peer governance and production processes; and*
> *and the "pooling economy" that enables collective ownership and management.*

It is customary for many city governments to be ignorant of the economics and social effects of network platform businesses, or to uncritically embrace "disruption" as a great advance for humanity. The CoR statement is quite different in tone and sophistication. It does not simply celebrate the new tech platforms. It notes that many of them are enabling a "reverse transformation or transition in some sectors of the current economic model to long-standing economic traditions and economic models," such as cooperatives, the social and solidarity economy, handicraft production, and commons.

Rather than welcoming any sweeping tech innovation as progress, the CoR intelligently urges the EU the EU to think about basic "design principles" for policies governing the sharing economy. Here in the US, it's every city and occupational sector for oneself, each fighting against the venture capital-funded giants who seem intent on bulldozing past any democratic accountability or "archaic" protections of workers, consumers or the general public (because "disruption" is necessarily good).

Let me readily concede that Uber is a far more convenient and inexpensive alternative to the traditional regulated taxi monopolies. The latter are often slow, unresponsive and averse to change, while Uber rides can be much easier to secure and cheaper. But much of Uber's economic viability comes from evading traditional worker and consumer protections, using data and algorithms to drive down wages, and aggressive lobbying to overcome regulators.

What the CoR proposes is a more thoughtful, rigorous and transparent process for considering the entire range of effects from tech-driven "disruptions." It wants a more serious, documented reckoning of net social and economic gains, to make sure that the "disruptions" are not simply the result of consolidating market power and shifting benefits to private interests from workers, public safety, the environment, social well-being and democratic accountability.

For example, the CoR proposes that EU policymaking not just focus on "the commercial and consumer aspects of the sharing economy while leaving aside the non-commercial and commons-based approaches." Just because the benefits of commons are not monetary, or cannot be easily quantified, is no reason to conclude that commons may not be more socially beneficial forms for meeting people's needs. For example, "platform cooperativism," in which a city government assures open standards, open competition, and data-sharing, could provide greater public benefit than a sector-dominating network platform company.

Thus, the CoR wants the European Commission to analyze and define the different forms of the sharing economy, and to take a sectoral approach in any regulation of the "sharing economy" so that the legal and institutional frameworks for regulation are appropriate. It also endorses the idea of regional autonomy in regulating the sharing economy, consistent with the principle of subsidiarity – governance at the smallest feasible level.

In terms of designing policy structures for the sharing economy, the CoR urges that:

Policies consider "all possible positive and negative impacts," including tax avoidance, unfair competition and violations of local and regional regulation. Policymakers should also consider the effects on "environmental regulation, social cohesion, equality and social justice, sound land use [and] urban governance."

"Social economy effects on personal economic security and social welfare must be thoroughly scrutinized," because the social economy may be giving rise to "a new social class, the collaborative class, that needs social and economic safeguards."

Data collection from sharing economy platforms "need to be open source as much as possible," and should "build in the platform technical mechanisms to feed public, relevant but not sensitive or strategic data to LRAs [local and regional authorities]. This is necessary because "free access to the market for newcomers needs to be guaranteed."

"Trust and reputation must be accurately and independently managed" via regulation, certification or third-party arbitration, or through peer review.

The CoR statement is far-sighted in calling for greater coordination among various EU departments to ensure that policies are consistent. It also urges that public administrators support the consolidation of a "collaborative institutional ecosystem" in its policy approaches, so that the general, common interests of everyone is taken into account. In other words, the Invisible Hand won't do the job.

The final, adopted opinion European Committee of the Regions is available here in English and in Italian. Additional information on the opinion is available on the Opinion Factsheet page on the CoR website, which also gives access to the opinion in other language versions as they become available.

I heartily recommend the CoR statement as a great place for other states, provinces and municipalities to grapple with the far-reaching challenges of platform enterprises. There's an important role for law and policy to play, especially in protecting the common good and vulnerable individuals and in fostering commons-based alternatives of equal or greater benefit. But achieving these goals will require a new sophistication about platform economics and their social impacts, and innovative regulatory approaches

Appendix D

Volunteering / Internship at SOHOland: Job description

(1) Meetup Activities / Events
a. *Organize Meetup sessions / events*
b. *Attend meetup sessions organized by third parties*
c. *Related events (on-line or off-line): Tribe / Neotribe related*

(2) Office Procedures / Social Media / Promotions
a. *Social Media updates, aiming for Tribe / Neotribe*
b. *Postings on websites, blogs, forum, groups etc.*
c. *Promotional or marketing of Short-term room rental etc.*

(3) House-keeping
a. *General Cleaning (rooms, kitchen, bathrooms, lounge)*
b. *Laundry of bedsheets etc. etc.*

(4) Seminars / Courses / Training
a. *Short courses / training (revenue-sharing: 70:30 in favor of trainer)*
b. *Preview sessions (on-line or off-line) and editing of e-book (in progress)*

(A) Working Hours and off-days (Highly flexible)
a. *Working hours per week maximum: 20 hours (Flexi-time)*
b. *Off-days: Saturdays and Sundays & gazette public holidays (except organized events or functions)*

(B) Food allowance / Subsidies / Accommodation

a. *Daily food allowance / subsidy of RM….. only*

b. *Private room accommodation will be provided*

c. *Therefore the weekly payment will be RM….. only*

(C) Legality and responsibility

a. *This is not an employer-employee relationship*

b. *This is not a contract of Joint Venture / Partnership (other than courses / workshop etc.)*

c. *Each party shall act in accordance to terms / conditions contained herein and no other claims / costs whatsoever will be entertained except on compassion ground.*

Commencing Date:

Finishing Date (Tentative):

Signed: SOHOLAND

  Volunteer / Intern

Appendix E

POSITIVE REAL ESTATE

- Best investment strategies (Sharing Economy & Block-chain)
- Best properties in any market (Sociable Home: SoHo)
- Use property to enrich personal life (Own it and live it!)
- m-Property Chain / m-Nation (Spread & Scale It)

This is the best combination of Life Portfolio (Own It) and Portfolio Life (Live It) Property Chain (Scale it)!

Positive Real Estate

. **Best investment strategies (Sharing Economy & Block-chain)**

. **Best properties in any market (Sociable Home: SoHo)**

. **Use property as Life Portfolio (Own It) and Portfolio Life (Live It)**

. **mini-Property Chain (Spread & Scale It)**

Appendix F

Social proof and references

This was my first time couch-surfing & the reviews for Eric as a host are very accurate. He has a lovely home, and he was very knowledgeable about things to do throughout the city. There were 2 other solo travelers there at the time that I stayed, and I felt like we were all part of a community because of his home/work/play/travel philosophy & lifestyle. My stay was exactly what I had hoped couchsurfing to be like. Kuala Lumpur is a beautiful city, and I recommend Eric as a host.

I stayed with Eric for two weeks to have a break of my travels and found the perfect place with everything someone could need, comfy bed, desk to work from, kitchen, chilled vive, good conversation, nice jungle walks, swimming pool and occasion to meet other great couch-surfers and digital nomads sharing their experience and getting away from the big city.

I stayed with Eric during my short stay in Kuala Lumpur. I've read his profile and I was so curious in his project that I've send him a request. He hosted me for 2 nights and told me everything about his project. Very interesting and such a devotion! Between organizing workshops and working on his project, he still found the time to show his CS-ers around and take them to the city. Eric, thank you for hosting me!

As you can already tell from his references, Eric is a truly seasoned couch-surfer. Even though I stayed at his place for just two days, I feel that I learned an incredible amount (both at the time and for later research!) from speaking to him and the others there: in particular about the lean economy and China's Belt and Road. He's very well up to date with new technologies and recommended me a slew of interesting websites to check out to upkeep my nomadic lifestyle.

He also took his intern and I to a jungle waterfall and a hot spring just outside of the city: a great taste of Malaysian wildlife! I've already recommended him to some friends visiting KL. You shouldn't miss the opportunity to meet him. He'll definitely inspire you with his ideas, and may just help you get on the career ladder or start your own business via his projects!

Eric is a legend in KL's community – and for great reasons above having hosted the most guests. Where should I start? First, Eric is extremely accommodating: my surf dates changed due to my schedule change, first shortened from seven nights to two, then after 2 nights I needed 2 extra nights, Eric never hesitated.

Second, Eric has great system going, from the detailed directions, his special co-living-working set up, your own keys, to all the places he'd take you and get the best out of your KL journey. I regret that I missed the jungle hike, but I'll always remember the hot-spring night, along with another guest (Eric always has the best guests! :D) I've been with CS since 2006, and I can honestly say that Eric has perfected the CS model to be a most rewarding and comfortable experience.

Last but not least, Eric stays in my CS family and bring his guests to my own events too. He personifies what's best about CS: strangers become lifelong friends and family, we learn from each other and grow, then we spread our CS spirit further to the world.

Thank you Eric, for sharing your wisdom and insights. For your enthusiasm for life. And for your precious friendship.

Hypercube @ SOHOLAND featured in Russian language at novy.tv

Appendix G

The 12-Element in the Hypercube

There are 12 distinct elements in the Hypercube as illustrated and summarized below.... This section should be read in conjunction with the respective relevant Chapters:

(1) Co-working
   a. Full facilities Business Centre on-site
   b. High-speed Broadband WiFi
   c. Remote working / E-commerce / digital nomads
   d. Lean Start-up / Incubator / Mentoring etc.

(2) Co-Living
   a. Week-end Retreat / Therapeutic Sanctuary
   b. Guest accommodation
   c. Social / Bachelor Mess
   d. Home-stay Program e.g. AirBnB

(3) The Commons
   a. Sharing Economy
   b. Collaborative Consumption
   c. Solidarity Economy
   d. Generative Shared Ownership

(4) Office-in-every-Home
   a. Personal and Family Finance Planning & Management
   b. Personal Development & Retirement Planning
   c. Personal Big Data: Predict and Prefigure
   d. Data-Information-Knowledge –Wisdom

(5) Sociable Home
   a. Great Socializer
   b. Great Equalizer
   c. Voluntary Simplicity
   d. Sanctuary & Support Network

(6) Systems Design
   a. Systems Thinking
   b. Systems Living
   c. Systems Being
   d. We are all "Holons"

(7) Estate Engine
   a. Why Real Estate Investment
   b. Property Cycle
   c. Understanding Property Auctions
   d. Due Diligence and Finding the Jewel

(8) Live
   a. Primary Residence as Consumption
   b. Secondary Home as Investment
   c. The Third Place as Social Condenser
   d. Your Most Powerful Personal Space

(9) Work
   a. Future of Work
   b. The Gig Economy
   c. Down-Shifting
   d. Half-Farmer & Half-X

(10) Travel
   a. Travel & Holiday Exchange
   b. Cultural & Work Exchange
   c. Couch-surfing & Hosting
   d. HelpX and Workaway

(11) Learn
   a. Life-Long-Learning & Skills Exchange
   b. Workshops & Seminars
   c. Life Coaching & Mentoring
   d. DIY and Open-source Fab-Lab etc.

(12) Play
   a. Entertainment & Relaxation / Recreation
   b. Pay cheque is Play-Cheque
   c. Life Journey should be "Play": Free, Fun and Fulfilling
   d. Meaning of Life and Meaning of Lite.

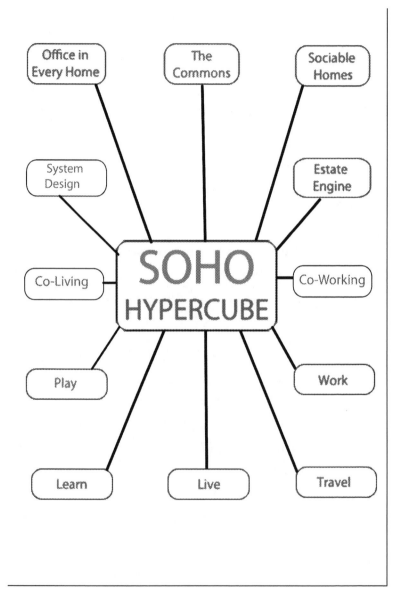

Office in Every Home

The Commons

Sociable Homes

System Design

Estate Engine

Co-Living

SOHO HYPERCUBE

Co-Working

Play

Work

Learn

Live

Travel

Appendix H

The Evolution of the Third Choice / Hypercube

The development of the Third Choice in the form of the Hypercube can be viewed chronologically, philosophically and physically....

Physically, the Hypercube is a Third Place (where First Place= Primary Residence, Second Place=Office or Work place, Third Place=SOHO, Small Office Home office etc.). The Third Choice is the decision to start owning and using the Third Place and its associated eco-system of Live-Work-Travel-Learn-Play. The different forms of SOHO (SOHO1 /SOHO2/ SOHO3 / SOHO4 etc.) could also be viewed as the physical and philosophical variances.

Chronologically, the Third Choice can be viewed as development of the Body / Mind / Spirit realms, involving personal development, productivity or business development, entrepreneurial development, leading to self-actualization and cosmic transcendence, represented by different levels of "success" such as, corporate (idolatrous), cognitive (inquisitive) and cosmic (integrative).

In the earlier stages of the development of the Hypercube, the business model is necessarily extractive, while the later stages will evolve into something generative or regenerative.

The Third Choice will therefore be a disruptive innovation and behavior change.

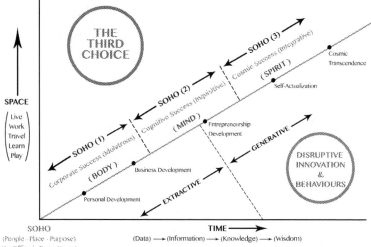

SPACE

(Live
Work
Travel
Learn
Play)

THE
THIRD
CHOICE

SOHO (3)
Cosmic Success (Integrative)
(SPIRIT)

Cosmic
Transcendence

SOHO (2)
Cognitive Success (Inquisitive)
(MIND)

Self-Actualization

SOHO (1)
Corporate Success (Adulatrous)
(BODY)

Entrepreneurship
Development

GENERATIVE

DISRUPTIVE
INNOVATION
&
BEHAVIOURS

Business Development

EXTRACTIVE

Personal Development

SOHO
(People · Place · Purpose)
(An-Office-in-Every-Home)
(Sociable Home)

TIME ➝

(Data) ⟶ (Information) ⟶ (Knowledge) ⟶ (Wisdom)

Appendix I

SOHO Hypercube as Social Business

The SOHO Hypecube is a social business or enterprise, as it contains both the social and the business aspects or elements.

The business element refers to the Recurrent Revenues (such as Co-working /Co-living spaces, workshops, training and publishing, property agency etc.) and Capital Gains or Appreciation (derived from fit / flip of auctioned properties, generative ownership and social franchise).

The social element refers to the community building effort in creating the Commons and related "commoning" activities, such as creating "Equity / Equality" (shared ownership), the required "Governance" (consensus management / cooperative format), to attaining Sovereignty (personal freedom and independence via lean start-ups etc.) to achieve Sustainability (the Triple Bottom Line of caring for Profit-People-Planet).

This is the Third Choice of the Commons, after Capitalism and Communism / Socialism.

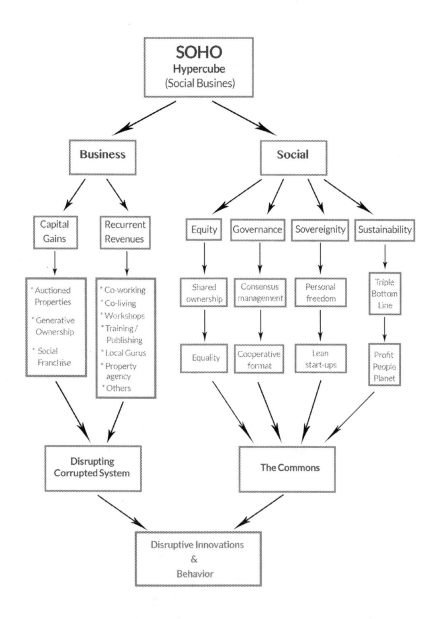

Appendix J

Trinity of Hypercube

Hypercube is a Trinity of Sharing Economy / LEAN Logic / Ethical Design. It is also a Social Business based on Sharing Economy (Co-Working& Co-Living), Ethical Design (Human scale & humane) and LEAN Logic (minimum costs, maximum participation and benefits).

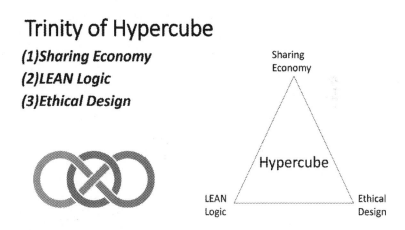

There are many things that have adopted the LEAN LOGIC (by Dr. David Fleming) principles, such as Lean Education, Lean Economics, Lean Food, Lean Health, Lean Household, Lean Production, Lean Startup etc. etc.

Emerging value is contingent on the production, and growth of community (instead of the production and growth of material wealth). Value is no longer compressed into "price". Ethics are now taken into equal consideration, because they are needed to sustain community, which is the emerging root of "value". Communities depend on ethics for cohesion / sustainability via Ethical Design (promoted by Aral and his team at ind.ie)

This Ethical Design is very much in line with being decentralized, localized, human scale and "small is beautiful" (or being LEAN), environmental friendly and sustainable ... fully in sync with the practice of the Commons. Ultimately, it is the pleasant and delightful experience (or "Play") generated by such design that is most valued and appreciated.

This is the core theme behind Hypercube @ SOHOland a.k.a LEAN Property Chain, eventually employing the Blockchain Technology (work-in-progress).

Appendix K

LEAN Property and LEAN Startup

* **LEAN PROPERTY: Minimum acquisition cost, but not low cost, maximum benefits (RICH Functionally, Socially, Culturally and spiritually) or best described in Chinese as "精益房產" vs. LEAN Startup "精益創業".**

Planning to buy an AFFORDABLE HOME to stay in … Don't! … Because you will become another consumer making a conspicuous consumption at this stage of life, possibly turning yourself a slave to your bank.

Be Wise ….Get a LEAN PROPERTY, instead…. You become a "prosumer" (producer and consumer), creating a lean startup business for yourself and owning the LEAN Property at the same time, on course to become mini-property-tycoon and much more (such as health, wealth and happiness) in the near future.

Affordable Home is not necessarily the answer. LEAN Property could well be, especially as Lean Startup… because your consumption (as user of the property) can be skillfully turned into your production / business / investment (i.e. as a Lean Startup business). This is made possible by our project's eco-system.

Therefore, owning a LEAN Property is equivalent to having a LEAN Startup business … killing two birds with one stone, so to speak.... solving unemployment ("looking for a job") and property ownership ("searching for an Affordable Home").

LEAN Property is therefore also a LEAN Startup business.

LEAN Startup vs. LEAN Property

LEAN Startup (精益創業)

- *Why look for a job when you can do a LEAN Startup (Business)?*
- *We are incubating LEAN Startup & LEAN Properties*

LEAN Property (精益房產)

- *Why look for an Affordable Homes aimlessly when you can immediately start owning a LEAN Property easily?*
- *LEAN Property is not "Low Cost", but LEAN (RICH functionally, socially, and culturally)*
- *LEAN Property as LEAN startup*

Appendix L

The L.E.A.N Collaborative

Do I have an "**Elevator Pitch**" for the Hypercube project? Yes…. Here is one of my shortest versions to date:

What am I doing? I am promoting LEAN PROPERTY / LEAN STARTUP or The L.E.A.N Collaborative in the form of a Social Business based on Sharing Economy (Co-Working & Co-Living), Ethical Design (Human Scale & Humane) and LEAN Logic (minimum costs, maximum participation and benefits)... promoting L.E.A.N (Lifestyle. Education. Asset. Network) collaboratively.

Lifestyle = Live-Work-Travel-Learn-Play eco-system rooted in ethical design

Education = LEAN Logic for sustainability, resilience and ethos

Asset = LEAN Properties or co-owned property chain of Hypercubes

Network = Sharing Community or Commons

The L.E.A.N Collaborative

(Lifestyle. Education. Asset. Network)

- **Lifestyle** (Live-Work-Travel-Learn-Play eco-system rooted in ethical design)
- **Education** (LEAN Logic for sustainability & resilience & ethics)
- **Asset** (LEAN Properties or co-owned Property chain of Hypercubes)
- **Network** (Sharing Community or Commons of Ethical Economy)

Note: Current and most physical manifestation is the "ASSET" aspect (in the form of LEAN Property or Co-Living and LEAN Startup or Co-Working)

Note: Current and most physical manifestation is the "ASSET" aspect (in the form of LEAN Property or Co-living space and LEAN Startup or Co-working space).

Endnotes

1. Ray Oldenburg. 1989. *The Great Good Place*. New York: Paragon Hous
2. Dom Nozzi. Dom's Plan B Blog. 2009. "What Is A "Third Place," And Why Are They Important?". https://domz60.wordpress. com/2009/01/02/what-is-a-third-place-and-why-are-they-important/.
3. Oldenburg. *The Great Good Place*.
4. Spaces, Project. 2016. "The Power Of 10+: Applying Placemaking At Every Scale - Project For Public Spaces". *Project For Public Spaces*. http:// www.pps.org/reference/the-power-of-10/.
5. "Commons". 2016. *Wikipedia*. Accessed February 21. https:// en.wikipedia.org/wiki/Commons.
6. Bollier, David. Bollier.org. 2016. "The Commons, Short And Sweet | David Bollier". http://bollier.org/commons-short-and-sweet.
7. Commons Rising. 2016. "About - Commons Rising". http:// commonsrising.uk.
8. Jessica Reeder. 2016. "Hacking Home: Coliving Reinvents The Commune For A Networked Age". *Shareable*. http://www.shareable. net/blog/hacking-home-coliving-reinvents-the-commune-for-a-networked-age.
9. Aaron Antonovsky. 1980. *Health, Stress, And Coping*. San Francisco: Jossey-Bass Publishers.
10. Encore.org. 2016. "Home - Encore.Org". http://encore.org/.
11. Lynda Gratton. 2011. *The Shift*. London: Collins.
12. Lynda Gratton. Apconsult.co.uk,. 2016. "The Changing Shape of Jobs: Work the Shift". http://www.apconsult.co.uk/executive-coaching-and-development/Lynda-Gratton-changing-shape-of-jobs.html.
13. Slowmovement.com,. 2016. "Downshifting Joins The Slow Movement". http://www.slowmovement.com/downshifting.php.
14. Slowmovement.com,. 2016. "Seachange And Downshifting In The Slow Movement". http://www.slowmovement.com/seachange.php.
15. Shiomi, Naoki. 2006. *Ban Nong Ban X De Sheng Huo*. Taibei Shi: Tian xia yuan jian chu ban gu fen you xian gong si.
16. Seung, Sebastian. 2010. "I Am My Connectome". *Ted.Com.* http://www.ted.com/talks/ sebastian seung?utm source=newsletter weekly 2010-09-

29&utm_campaign=newsletter_weekly&utm_medium=email.

17. Tomales Bay Institute. 2006. *Commons Rising*. A Report To Owners. Minneapolis, MN

18. Andreas Weber. 2013. *Enlivenment: Towards A Fundamental Shift In The Concepts Of Nature, Culture And Politics*. Berlin: Heinrich Böll Stiftung. https://www.boell.de/en/2013/02/01/enlivenment-towards-fundamental-shift-concepts-nature-culture-and-politics.

19. Andreas Weber. *Enlivenment: Towards A Fundamental Shift*

20. Marshall B Rosenberg. 2003. *The Heart Of Social Change*. Encinitas, CA: PuddleDancer Press.

21. David Brooks. 2014. "Should You Live For Your Résumé ... Or Your Eulogy?". In *TED Conference*. https://www.ted.com/talks/david_brooks_should_you_live_for_your_resume_or_your_eulogy?language=en#t-285362.

22. Lars Tornstam. 2005. *Gerotranscendence*. New York: Springer Pub. Co.

23. Erik H Erikson and Joan M Erikson. 1997. *The Life Cycle Completed*. New York: W.W. Norton.

24. Peter Checkland. 2002. *Systems Thinking, Systems Practice*. Chichester: Wiley.

25. Kathia Laszlo. 2011. "Beyond Systems Thinking: The Role Of Beauty And Love In The Transformation Of Our World". Presentation, 55th Meeting of the International Society for the Systems Sciences at the University of Hull, U.K.

26. Ken Honda. 2006. *Eight Steps To Happiness & Prosperity*. Japan: Sunmark Publishing.

Bibliography

Antonovsky, Aaron. 1980. *Health, Stress, And Coping*. San Francisco: Jossey-Bass Publishers.

Bollier, David. Bollier.org. 2016. "The Commons, Short And Sweet | David Bollier". http://bollier.org/commons-short-and-sweet.

Brooks, David. 2014. "Should You Live For Your Résumé ... Or Your Eulogy?". In *TED Conference*. https://www.ted.com/talks/david_brooks_should_you_live_for_your_resume_or_your_eulogy?language=en#t-285362.

Checkland, Peter. 2002. *Systems Thinking, Systems Practice*. Chichester: Wiley.

"Commons". 2016. *Wikipedia*. Accessed February 21. https://en.wikipedia.org/wiki/Commons.

Commons Rising. 2016. "About - Commons Rising". http://commonsrising.uk.

David Fleming, *LEAN LOGIC (A Dictionary for the Future and How to Survive It)*, Edited by Shaun Chamberlin. 2016

Encore.org. 2016. "Home - Encore.Org". http://encore.org/.

Erikson, Erik H, and Joan M Erikson. 1997. *The Life Cycle Completed*. New York: W.W. Norton.

Gratton, Lynda. 2011. *The Shift*. London: Collins.

Gratton, Lynda. Apconsult.co.uk. 2016. "The Changing Shape of Jobs: Work the Shift". http://www.apconsult. co.uk/executive-coaching-and-development/Lynda-Gratton-changing-shape-of-jobs.html.

Honda, Ken. 2006. *Eight Steps To Happiness & Prosperity.* Japan: Sunmark Publishing.

Laszlo, Kathia. 2011. "Beyond Systems Thinking: The Role Of Beauty And Love In The Transformation Of Our World". Presentation, 55th Meeting of the International Society for the Systems Sciences at the University of Hull, U.K.

Nozzi, Dom, Dom's Plan B Blog. 2009. "What Is A " Third Place," And Why Are They Important?". https://domz60.wordpress.com/2009/01/02/ what-is-a-third-place-and-why-are-they-important/.

Oldenburg, Ray. 1989. *The Great Good Place.* New York: Paragon House.

Reeder, Jessica. 2016. "Hacking Home: Coliving Reinvents The Commune For A Networked Age". *Shareable.* http://www. shareable.net/blog/hacking-home-coliving-reinvents-the-commune-for-a-networked-age.

Rosenberg, Marshall B. 2003. *The Heart Of Social Change.* Encinitas, CA: PuddleDancer Press.

Seung, Sebastian. 2010. "I Am My Connectome". *Ted.Com.* http://www.ted.com/talks/ sebastian_seung?utm_source=newsletter_weekly_2010-09-29&utm_campaign=newsletter_weekly&utm_medium=email.

Shiomi, Naoki. 2006. *Ban Nong Ban X De Sheng Huo.* Taibei Shi: Tian xia yuan jian chu ban gu fen you xian gong si.

Slowmovement.com. 2016. "Downshifting Joins The Slow Movement". http://www.slowmovement.com/ downshifting.php.

Slowmovement.com. 2016. "Seachange And Downshifting In The Slow Movement". http://www.slowmovement.com/ seachange.php.

Spaces, Project. 2016. "The Power Of 10+: Applying Placemaking At Every Scale - Project For Public Spaces". *Project For Public Spaces.* http://www.pps.org/reference/ the-power-of-10/.

Tomales Bay Institute. 2006. *Commons Rising.* A Report To Owners. Minneapolis, MN.

Tornstam, Lars. 2005. *Gerotranscendence.* New York: Springer Pub. Co.

Weber, Andreas. 2013. "From Enlivenment To Shared Livelihoods: The Emergence Of A Commons-Based Economy". *Shareable.* http://www.shareable.net/blog/from-enlivenment-to-shared-livelihoods-the-emergence-of-a-commons-based-economy.

Weber, Andreas. 2013. *Enlivenment: Towards A Fundamental Shift In The Concepts Of Nature, Culture And Politics*. Berlin: Heinrich Böll Stiftung. https://www.boell.de/en/2013/02/01/enlivenment-towards-fundamental-shift-concepts-nature-culture-and-politics.

Printed in the United States
By Bookmasters